CASE STUDIES
OF NONPROFIT
ORGANIZATIONS
AND VOLUNTEERS

This book is part of the Peter Lang Media and Communication list.
Every volume is peer reviewed and meets
the highest quality standards for content and production.

PETER LANG
New York • Bern • Frankfurt • Berlin
Brussels • Vienna • Oxford • Warsaw

CASE STUDIES
OF NONPROFIT
ORGANIZATIONS
AND VOLUNTEERS

EDITED BY

JENNIFER MIZE SMITH
AND MICHAEL W. KRAMER

PETER LANG
New York • Bern • Frankfurt • Berlin
Brussels • Vienna • Oxford • Warsaw

Library of Congress Cataloging-in-Publication Data

Case studies of nonprofit organizations and volunteers /
edited by Jennifer Mize Smith, Michael W. Kramer.
pages cm
Includes bibliographical references and index.
1. Nonprofit organizations—Management—Case studies.
2. Non-governmental organizations—Management—Case studies.
3. Voluntarism—Management—Case studies. 4. Volunteers—Case studies.
I. Mize Smith, Jennifer. II. Kramer, Michael W.
HD62.6.C268   658'.048—dc23   2014042553
ISBN 978-1-4331-2690-1 (hardcover)
ISBN 978-1-4331-2689-5 (paperback)
ISBN 978-1-4539-1483-0 (e-book)

Bibliographic information published by **Die Deutsche Nationalbibliothek**.
Die Deutsche Nationalbibliothek lists this publication in the "Deutsche
Nationalbibliografie"; detailed bibliographic data are available
on the Internet at http://dnb.d-nb.de/.

The paper in this book meets the guidelines for permanence and durability
of the Committee on Production Guidelines for Book Longevity
of the Council of Library Resources.

Printed in the United States of America

To the many individuals who serve nonprofit
organizations in multiple ways to make lives
better and communities stronger

Preface

Given the increasing presence of nonprofit organizations and their impact upon American society, it is not surprising that colleges and universities are recognizing the need to offer courses and programs to train current and future employees, volunteers, and supporters of the nonprofit sector. However, despite the proliferation in nonprofit courses and programs, much of the current nonprofit literature is prescriptive and aimed toward practitioners.

In contrast, this book takes a more descriptive approach and is designed for those who teach undergraduate and graduate courses related to the nonprofit sector and civil society organizations, including nonprofit management, nonprofit communication, voluntarism, and philanthropic studies. Each case study is a unique teaching tool that explores multiple organizational and communicative issues for readers to ponder, question, and discuss. Multiple stakeholder perspectives are represented, along with multiple concepts.

Perhaps more importantly, each chapter tells a story that reflects the kind of work—both rewarding and challenging—that goes on every day in nonprofit organizations across America. At the very least, we hope that readers will take away a greater understanding of nonprofit and volunteer work. Greater still, we hope that readers will see themselves in one of the stories and be inspired to pursue their own role in a nonprofit context as a leader, volunteer, or donor.

ACKNOWLEDGMENTS

We want to thank Mary Savigar, senior acquisitions editor for Peter Lang Publishing, who saw the need for a pedagogical resource for all those who teach nonprofit-related courses. We appreciate her confidence in our proposal and her guidance throughout the publishing process. We also thank our families and colleagues who took interest in our project and who supported our efforts along the way.

Finally, we give a special thanks to the authors who contributed their work to create such a valuable collection of case studies. These chapters represent but a small sampling of their research, and we appreciate the countless hours of time and energy they have devoted to furthering our understanding of nonprofit and volunteer contexts.

The Editors
Jennifer Mize Smith
Michael W. Kramer

Table of Contents

Introduction

An Introduction to Nonprofit Organizations and Volunteers

JENNIFER MIZE SMITH
Western Kentucky University

MICHAEL W. KRAMER
University of Oklahoma

A couple serves meals at the local soup kitchen sponsored by their church. A father joins the Parent Teacher Association. A mother coaches her son's soccer team as part of the local parks and recreation league. An employee participates in a "give back to the community day" at his workplace by planting trees. Every day across America and around the world, numerous individuals contribute to and benefit from the important work of nonprofit organizations (NPOs).

Nonprofit organizations seek to fill the gap in needs not met by either the private or governmental sectors of society. Consequently, NPOs offer an array of goods and services—from providing basic necessities such as food, clothing, shelter, and healthcare, to enhancing education, recreation, culture, aesthetics, and the arts. By and large, nonprofit organizations improve the quality of life in our communities.

The United States has long enjoyed a thriving nonprofit sector. The American Revolution ushered in not only a new republic, but also a new face of philanthropy. With the separation of church and state, the need for new sources of social support sparked a proliferation of voluntary associations and charitable organizations (Gross, 2003). The vast and varied work of nonprofit organizations makes it difficult to construct a universal definition of NPOs. However, most would agree with Salamon and Anheier (1992) that nonprofit organizations typically share five key characteristics: (1) formal—some degree of formal organization or system of operation; (2) private—institutionally separate from government; (3) non-profit-distributing—returning any profits that are generated back into the organization's mission, rather than giving profits to owners or directors; (4) self-governing—constructing their own system of governance; and (5) voluntary—involving some degree of voluntary participation.

Nonprofit organizations may consist entirely of paid employees or entirely of volunteers, but most have a combination of the two, thus stretching traditional conceptions of organizational "member." The task of defining a volunteer is equally challenging. Most scholars agree that a volunteer is someone who generally meets these three criteria: he/she (1) performs some task of free will; (2) receives no remuneration; and (3) acts altruistically to benefit others (Handy et al., 2000; Lewis, 2013). Although this definition seems fairly straightforward, the definition is somewhat problematic. For example, the courts sometimes sentence individuals to do community service, and students are sometimes required to do service learning to meet course or graduation requirements. In these cases, they are likely to be called volunteers, and their work is indistinguishable from that performed by other volunteers. However, it is difficult to describe their participation as totally free will, although they may have a choice of what particular service they perform. Other volunteers receive free admissions to events, such as volunteer ushers (Scott & Stephens, 2009); technically, they receive remuneration for their time and service. Despite these and other exceptions, the three criteria mentioned are useful in shaping our notion of *volunteer*.

There are a variety of reasons why we should study and learn about nonprofit organizations and volunteers, the first of which is the sheer size of the nonprofit sector. As of 2010, nonprofit organizations numbered approximately 2.3 million in the US alone; they contributed 5.5% or $804.8 billion to the country's gross domestic product; and public charities reported $1.51 trillion in revenue (Blackwood, Roeger, & Pettijohn, 2012).

The degree to which nonprofit organizations are financially supported also warrants some attention. Despite the sluggish economy that plagued the early part of the 21st century, Americans' charitable giving increased a fourth consecutive year in 2013. According to the Giving USA 2014 report, the $335.17 billion donated to charity is nearing the all-time giving highs experienced just before the latest recession. Individuals continue to give the lion's share of philanthropic dollars, collectively contributing 72% of all charitable gifts.

Individuals are not only opening their wallets to support NPOs; they are also giving their time. A 2012 report prepared by the National Center for Charitable Statistics notes that in 2011, approximately 26.8% of adults in the US gave time to a charitable organization, contributing 15.2 billion volunteer hours valued at approximately $296.2 billion. On a daily basis in 2011, 6% of the US population volunteered an average of 2.84 hours (Blackwood et al., 2012). Other studies indicate that the typical volunteer in the US contributes 4.5 hours per week to various NPOs, including community, religious, recreational, and arts organizations

(Hooghe, 2003). These volunteers represent a wide range of demographics who volunteer at different rates. In the US, women volunteer more often than men (28.4% to 22.2%); middle-aged people are more likely to volunteer than people in their early 20s (30.6% to 18.5%); married people volunteer at a higher rate (30.7%) than those never married (20%) or of other marital statuses (20.5%); college graduates volunteer at a higher rate than those with less education; and whites volunteer at a higher rate than other ethnic groups. The largest group of volunteers participate in religious organizations (33%), followed by educational/youth services (25.6%) and social/community services (14.7%) (Bureau of Labor Statistics, 2014). These numbers indicate that volunteering is a significant part of the lives of many individuals in the US.

Giving and volunteering are indeed staples of the American culture. And thanks to those who give their time and resources, the nonprofit sector has weathered economic boons and lows and continues to impact lives in important and meaningful ways. The increasing amount of time, effort, and dollars given to charitable endeavors suggests that we, as teachers, scholars, and practitioners, *should* be studying nonprofit organizations and volunteers. More important than size and magnitude, however, is the impact of NPOs and the ways in which they make numerous lives easier, healthier, more interesting, and more enjoyable. Thus philanthropic contexts deserve greater attention and examination in our effort to understand how nonprofit work unfolds every day.

For many scholars, a useful starting point is to take traditional organizational concepts, often generated from studies in the for-profit sector, and "try them on" in a nonprofit context. We can then better understand the dynamics of nonprofit organizing and the ways in which they may inform and be informed by organizational communication theories. For example, it appears that the experiences of volunteers are in many ways similar to those of employees in for-profit businesses. Further examination of volunteers and NPOs can provide insights into the similarities and uniqueness of these two primary ways individuals participate in organizations.

To illustrate this, consider the process of joining an organization as a new employee or as a new volunteer. New employees must seek information to learn what to do and how to do it, to develop relationships with others, and to learn the organization's norms and culture (Miller & Jablin, 1991; Morrison, 1995). Similarly, new volunteers must develop communication channels to gain information, learn their job/tasks, create relationships with other organizational members, and make sense of the organization's culture (McComb, 1995). Yet, despite these similarities, there are some significant differences. Employees generally go through a process of anticipatory socialization before joining, become newcomers, perhaps full members and then eventually exit the organization (Jablin, 2001). By contrast, it is very common for volunteers to fluctuate between membership and nonmembership as a volunteer, take temporary leaves to manage other work-life issues, and perhaps return at a later date (Kramer, 2011).

The case studies that follow explore socialization and many other topics covered in a typical organizational communication, management, or human resource course; however, they focus on volunteers or employees of NPOs instead of employees of businesses and government agencies. By studying volunteers and NPO employees and comparing their experiences to those in government and for-profit businesses, we can learn more about participation in organizations in general and further our understanding of both employment and volunteering.

PREVIEW

The book is divided into eight sections. Each section focuses on a particular nonprofit stakeholder and illuminates issues and concepts that are salient to that group. Following an introduction to nonprofit organizations and volunteers (Chapter One), Section One denotes the difficult job of leading a nonprofit organization. Executive directors are often faced with important choices about organizational governance, policies (Williams, Chapter Two), and partnerships (Kindred and Petrescu, Chapter Three). Their decisions and actions may have long-term effects on those they serve (Huffman, Chapter Four), as well as their organization's identity and future support (Drumheller, Kinsky, and Gerlich, Chapter Five). As these cases clearly illustrate, executive directors have the difficult job of pursuing the NPO's best interests while simultaneously considering, negotiating, and serving the interests of multiple others, such as board members, clients, staff, volunteers, other NPOs, and funders.

In addition to executive directors, other staff members may also experience a number of challenges, as discussed in Section Two. While nonprofit work is rewarding in many ways, it can also be overwhelming. Staff members often work long hours with few resources (D'Enbeau and Kunkel, Chapter Six; Ginossar and Oetzel, Chapter Seven), which can lead to stress and burnout. The ongoing task of recruiting and retaining volunteers is never done (Peterson and McNamee, Chapter Eight). They may also face difficult ethical choices, such as how to stay true to clients, the organization's mission, and self (Anderson and Clair, Chapter Nine; Shuler, Chapter Ten). For many, a career in nonprofit work is much more than a job; it is a calling (Mize Smith et al., 2006), which likely intensifies both the highs and lows of their everyday work.

The cases in Section Three turn our attention to other nonprofit leaders—the Board of Directors. Most nonprofit boards are composed of volunteers who lend their time, expertise, and resources to provide leadership and governance to nonprofit organizations. Committing to join a nonprofit board can be a big decision

(Milburn and Hansen, Chapter Eleven), but after years of service, stepping down from a board can be equally difficult (Tye-Williams and Marshall, Chapter Twelve). Although meetings may not always go as planned (Jameson, Chapter Thirteen), Boards of Directors are charged with important tasks, such as hiring the executive director (Kramer, Chapter Fourteen), as well as garnering support and charting the overall direction of the organization (Violanti, Chapter Fifteen). The strength and effectiveness of board decisions are instrumental to the success of NPOs.

In addition to a Board of Directors, most nonprofit organizations rely to varying degrees on volunteers. Section Four offers a glimpse into some of their experiences. While volunteering can certainly be rewarding, it can also be frustrating, leaving volunteers to wonder if they really did any good (Zanin, Chapter Sixteen). Volunteers may also find themselves coming to terms with issues of individual and organizational identity (Lee and Baker, Chapter Seventeen) and even struggling to balance their volunteer work with other aspects of their lives (McAllum, Chapter Eighteen). At first glance, it might be easy to dismiss these issues, since a volunteer is not paid and therefore free to leave at any time. However, these cases demonstrate how seriously volunteers take their roles and how deeply they identify with the organizations they serve.

Section Five highlights a particular type of volunteer—those who take their time and talents across borders to serve internationally. The Peace Corps is perhaps one of the most well-known international volunteer organizations; yet even with its long history of success, volunteers' training does not completely prepare them for service in a foreign country (Fletcher and Hongmei Gao, Chapter Nineteen). There is much to be learned simply by doing (Kumar and Koenig, Chapter Twenty). Consequently, volunteers are left to make sense not only of cultural differences, but also of their own identities and beliefs.

There is no doubt that volunteers do vast amounts of important work both at home and abroad. But as important as they are, their work would not be possible without the support of donors. With 2.3 million NPOs in the US alone, the competition for charitable dollars is increasingly fierce. Not surprisingly, then, the art and science of fundraising is a growing profession, particularly in the area of education, which consistently ranks as the second most supported nonprofit subsector, second only to religious organizations (Giving USA Foundation, 2014). Section Six offers insight into the fundraising profession, particularly in higher education. Like other professionals, fundraisers and development officers have constructed their own metaphorical jargon, and while it has meaning to them, it can be challenging for newcomers to understand and navigate (Carver, Chapter Twenty-One). The professionalization of fundraising also poses interesting questions about one's loyalty to a cause or particular NPO versus the profession (Meisenbach and Rick, Chapter Twenty-Two). These and other issues are important to examine given the critical role of fundraising in maintaining and growing the nonprofit sector.

As nonprofit organizations struggle to find volunteers and donors, more and more are turning to corporations for support. Although corporations provided only 5% of total charitable contributions in 2013 (Giving USA Foundation, 2014), corporate partners offer important inroads to large groups of employees who are potential volunteers and donors. The cases in Section Seven illuminate the experiences of employees in companies across America who are asked to give and volunteer at work. While NPOs greatly benefit from employee volunteer programs (Satterlund and May, Chapter Twenty-Three) and workplace giving campaigns (Mize Smith, Chapter Twenty-Four), we must also consider the employees' perspective, including the potential consequences and problems that may arise when philanthropy is managerially constructed.

Finally, Section Eight reminds us of perhaps the most important nonprofit stakeholder group—service recipients. As mentioned previously, nonprofit organizations are created to fill societal needs that would otherwise go unmet. While every citizen benefits in some way from nonprofit programs and services, the populations most served are often stigmatized groups. The impoverished is one example of a social out-group, and yet they may be less different than perceived. Nonprofit organizations must look for ways to connect their clients with potential donors and volunteers (Payne, Mize Smith, and Newman, Chapter Twenty-Five). Increasing identification will likely increase support for the organization. Another stigmatized group is the unemployed, particularly middle-aged and older. While there are NPOs to assist them, even staff and volunteers may find it difficult to relate to clients' feelings and circumstances (Gist, Chapter Twenty-Six).

Together, these case studies offer a unique, behind-the-scenes view into the everyday experiences of various groups who make nonprofit organizing and organizations possible. As the stories unfold, you will get a glimpse of passion and joy, frustration and disappointment, commitment and resolve, and a range of other emotions as characters go about their work in and of nonprofits and volunteering. Without a doubt, the challenges they face and the choices they make have a monumental impact on lives, communities, and society.

NOTES TO INSTRUCTORS

Teaching with case studies is an excellent way to bring organizational concepts to life through stories and examples from outside the classroom. Few of our current resources (books, texts, handbooks) address the micro-level, data-based analysis of communication and other organizational issues in nonprofit, volunteer, and philanthropic contexts. We envision this book as a useful, empirically based resource for instruction that can be utilized in a variety of ways. Some instructors may prefer to use this text as the primary reading, introducing students to particular types of NPOs, as well as the unique characteristics of nonprofit organizations and volunteering. This resembles an inductive approach to teaching in which the specific case is examined first and then the discussion is used to develop and explain more general concepts and theories. For others, this book may serve as a secondary resource, providing examples of the concepts found in a primary text or journal articles. This resembles a deductive approach to teaching in which the concepts and theories are first defined in general and then applied to the specific cases in this book. Obviously, a combination of the two is also possible.

Each chapter presents a case that illustrates one or more issues related to nonprofit organizations and their stakeholders (i.e., managers, staff, boards, volunteers, donors, and service recipients). This casebook extends beyond a traditional managerial perspective to explore how numerous others, not just managers, experience, construct, negotiate, and make sense of the issues presented. The book is divided into sections based on our categorization of the most salient issues illustrated by each case. However, instructors may decide to use the cases to focus on decidedly different topics. For example, although we have included "Working Hard for Less Money?" (Chapter Twenty-Two) under the section on fundraising as a profession, you may prefer to use it to discuss the types and importance of peer relationships in the socialization process (Kram & Isabella, 1985). We encourage instructors to creatively use the cases for instruction based on their perceptions of the concepts that they illustrate.

Cases are open-ended such that a main character is faced with an unresolved question or issue. We encourage instructors to use the open-endedness to discuss some of the ambiguity and uncertainty that exists in organizational settings. These cases are designed to illustrate that uncertainty and ambiguity are common and often lead to making choices based on ethical principles. We encourage instructors to embrace this aspect of the cases.

To jump-start the discussion, a series of six to eight questions were designed by the case study authors to help students critically think about the particular nonprofit context, the organizational issues presented, the ways in which those issues could be addressed, whose interests are served, and potential consequences for the organization and its various stakeholders. Some discussion questions narrowly focus on specific case details and characters. Others encourage broader thinking by challenging readers to consider how concepts and perspectives might relate to other NPOs or compare to for-profit organizations.

To further aid with instruction, authors have defined key terms and suggested additional readings for further exploration of relevant concepts. While illuminating a particular nonprofit context, each chapter also addresses a broader conceptual or theoretical issue or framework of organizational studies. Consequently, the book provides more than just case studies of nonprofit organizations, but also addresses larger issues of organization and communication.

Although the book is primarily aimed toward those teaching nonprofit-related courses, we expect that nonprofit practitioners might also find it valuable. For those who currently manage or are seeking to start a nonprofit organization, this compilation of issues and challenges could be utilized for discussion, training, strategic planning, and organizational evaluation among staff, volunteers, and Boards of Directors. Admittedly, not every reader will work for a nonprofit organization, but most will be called upon to support them, and all will, knowingly or unknowingly, benefit from their services and the stronger communities they create.

NOTES TO STUDENTS

Case studies offer a valuable learning experience, and we encourage students to use them in a variety of ways. Within a few short pages, you are transported outside the classroom to engage in real organizations with real problems. The decisions that are made have real consequences for real people. Keep in mind that each case is based on empirical data. While some of the names and characters may have been fictionalized, the situations and dilemmas at hand reflect the everyday work of these NPOs and many like them across the country. We invite readers to question and critique the decisions and actions of case characters, to construct other possible alternatives, to craft different messages, and to envision subsequent moves and scenarios. What could the characters have done differently to address the issue? What would you have done in their shoes?

Each case is open-ended with a main character facing a choice or dilemma. You may be tempted to focus on what the "correct" action would be, as if there is one best choice to make. We encourage you to avoid this singular focus. Since some of the cases involve ethical choices, a best course of action likely indicates a particular ethic perspective rather than a correct decision. In other cases, it is impossible to evaluate the consequences of a particular decision: clearly choosing one leader over another will make a difference in an organization ("The Choice", Chapter Fourteen), but one choice is not inherently better than another—they are just different. So instead of trying to find the correct answer, we encourage you to reserve judgment when possible so that you broadly consider the possible positive and negative consequences of various alternatives.

We also encourage students to think about what the unique characteristic of *nonprofit-ness* brings to bear on the situation. What might be a similar scenario in a for-profit context? And if so, how might the situation have been handled differently? For example, would nonprofit staff act differently if they worked in a profit-making corporation? Would volunteers think or behave differently if they were paid staff? As mentioned previously, we have a lot to learn from comparing and contrasting the different sectors of our society. What we know of one sector may fruitfully inform, extend, or challenge what we know of another.

We hope that you will relate your own experiences to the experiences of the case study characters. Odds are you already have some experience with nonprofit organizations—probably more than you think. Some of you have donated to a nonprofit cause. Ever given blood to the Red Cross, bought Girl Scout cookies, or pitched a few coins in the Salvation Army buckets during the holidays? Many of you have served as a volunteer at some point. Ever tutored at the local Boys and Girls Club, participated in a mission trip, volunteered to coach a youth sports team, or sorted food at the local food bank? And all of you have benefited from nonprofit programs and services. That awesome play or concert you attended—it was likely provided by a nonprofit arts organization with volunteer ushers. Those pretty historic buildings you admire downtown? They were likely restored by a nonprofit preservation society. And the school you're attending? Albeit a public or private institution, it is likely a nonprofit educational entity that relies on volunteers and donations to support many of its programs. We encourage you to draw upon your own knowledge of NPOs and volunteering, apply what you know to analyze each case, and apply what you learn from each case to make sense of your own experiences. Not everything that you learn from the cases needs to be a concept or theory that will appear on a test. Valuable learning can occur that you can apply to your unique life situations—past, present, and future.

CONCLUSION

While this set of case studies is a valuable resource reflecting the important work in and of nonprofit organizing, it also reminds us that so much more is yet to be explored. Organizational and communication scholars are well poised not only to further examine extant concepts and theories in nonprofit and volunteering contexts, but also to develop new ideas and insights that may be uniquely related to the nuances of working and volunteering in the nonprofit sector. We applaud those who have seen the need for nonprofit scholarship and who have contributed to the research efforts in these areas. We hope this book extends the conversation and perhaps attracts new interest in better understanding nonprofit organizations and volunteers.

REFERENCES

Blackwood, A. S., Roeger, K. L., & Pettijohn, S. L. (2012). *The nonprofit sector in brief: Public charities, giving, and volunteering, 2012*. Washington, DC: Urban Institute. Retrieved from http://www.urban.org/UploadedPDF/412674-The-Nonprofit-Sector-in-Brief.pdf

Bureau of Labor Statistics. (2014). *Volunteering in the United States, 2010*. Washington, DC: US Government Printing Office. Retrieved from http://www.bls.gov/news.release/pdf/volun.pdf

Giving USA Foundation. (2014). Giving USA 2014: The annual report on philanthropy for the year 2013. Retrieved from http://store.givingusareports.org/

Gross, R. A. (2003). Giving in America: From charity to philanthropy. In L. J. Friedman & M. D. McGarvie (Eds.), *Charity, philanthropy, and civility in American history* (pp. 29–48). Cambridge, UK: Cambridge University Press.

Handy, F., Cnaan, R., Brudney, J., Ascoli, U., Meijs, L. M. P., & Ranade, S. (2000). Public perception of "who is a volunteer": An examination of the net-cost approach from a cross-cultural perspective. *Voluntas: International Journal of Voluntary and Nonprofit Organizations, 11*, 45–65. doi: 10.1023/A:1008903032393

Hooghe, M. (2003). Participation in voluntary associations and value indicators: The effect of current and previous participation experiences. *Nonprofit and Voluntary Sector Quarterly, 32*, 47–69.

Jablin, F. M. (2001). Organizational entry, assimilation, and disengagement/exit In F. M. Jablin & L. L. Putnam (Eds.), *The new handbook of organizational communication: Advances in theory, research, and methods* (pp. 732–818). Thousand Oaks, CA: Sage.

Kram, K. E., & Isabella, L. A. (1985). Mentoring alternatives: The role of peer relationships in career development. *Academy of Management Journal, 28*, 110–132.

Kramer, M. W. (2011). A study of voluntary organizational membership: The assimilation process in a community choir. *Western Journal of Communication, 75*, 52–74. doi:10.1080/10570314.2010. 536962

Lewis, L. K. (2013). An introduction to volunteers. In M. W. Kramer, L. K. Lewis, & L. M. Gossett (Eds.), *Volunteers and communciation: Studies in multiple contexts* (pp. 1–22). New York, NY: Peter Lang.

McComb, M. (1995). Becoming a travelers aid volunteer: Communication in socialization and training. *Communication Studies, 46*, 297–316. doi:10.1080/10510979509368458

Miller, V. D., & Jablin, F. M. (1991). Information seeking during organizational entry: Influences, tactics, and a model of the process. *Academy of Management Review, 16*, 92–120. doi:10.2307/258608

Mize Smith, J., Arendt, C., Lahman, J. B., Settle, G., & Duff, A. (2006). Framing the work of art: Spirituality and career discourse in the nonprofit arts sector [Special issue]. *Communication Studies, 57*, 25–46.

Morrison, E. W. (1995). Information usefulness and acquisition during organizational encounter. *Management Communication Quarterly, 9*, 131–155. doi:10.1177/0893318995009002001

Salamon, L. M., & Anheier, H. K. (1992). In search of the non-profit sector. I: The question of definitions. *Voluntas: International Journal of Voluntary and Nonprofit Organizations, 3*, 125–151. doi: 10.1007/BF01397770

Scott, C. R., & Stephens, K. K. (2009). It depends on who you're talking to …: Predictors and outcomes of situated measures of organizational identification. *Western Journal of Communication, 73*, 370–394. doi:10.1080/10570310903279075

Executive Director Dilemmas: Change, Collaboration, AND Crisis

CHAPTER TWO

Leading Change

An Examination of Communication Practices Aimed at Organizational Change*

ELIZABETH A. WILLIAMS

Colorado State University

Robert was in a reflective mood. It had been a year since he started as the executive director (ED) at Counties United to End Homelessness (CUEH), and he had just found a list he made his first day on the job detailing tasks he wanted to accomplish during his first year. CUEH was a nonprofit organization aimed at preventing and ending homelessness in a large metro area. The mission of CUEH was to facilitate, integrate, and track cooperative, community-wide, and regional systems of care for the homeless. Part of CUEH's role was to distribute millions of grant dollars to support the operations of homeless service providers.

Robert knew when he began his new position that if he did not get some alignment or partnership with the Board of Directors, he would experience difficulty. The board fired the previous ED after only six weeks, and before that, they were without an ED for five years. When Robert started his job, he was optimistic that he could be successful. He had worked with the homeless for years and had relationships across the community and in the local and state government. But most importantly, he really understood the issues that the organization faced.

As Robert looked at the year-old list, he recalled the many obstacles he faced when he joined CUEH. He had listed three major tasks he wanted to tackle: (1) changing the role of the board; (2) enacting system change; and (3) mobilizing volunteers to change beliefs.

First on his list had been to shift the role of the board. As a working board, members had been involved in and responsible for the day-to-day organizational operations during the five years it had been without an ED. With the absence of staff leadership, board members had divided the operational duties. Robert had known that, to be successful, he had to shift to a governing board model. Furthermore, he had suspected that this would be difficult for those who had been in the driver's seat.

Thinking back over the last year, Robert realized that the transition from a working to a governing board had gone smoother than expected. While some board members expressed resistance, Robert had honest conversations with them to explain that board members chairing committees created an uncomfortable dynamic between the board, staff, community volunteers, and other stakeholders. Eventually, board members accepted Robert's explanation, perhaps partly out of their exhaustion from working as both a governing and operating board—indeed, some seemed relieved to give up some responsibilities.

That is not to say that Robert had not acted strategically. He actively sought out neutral voices to join the board—voices reflecting the larger community. Time and time again, when he approached potential board members, they said, "But I don't know a lot about homelessness. I don't know about Continuums of Care and all of those technical aspects." To that Robert always responded, "I don't want you to. I want you to come in with fresh eyes, fresh ideas, not biased because you're not receiving grants through us. Homelessness isn't your mainstay of how you make a living. We need those outside voices and perspectives to go, 'This doesn't make sense,' or say, 'Why are you doing it this way?'" It was with this framing that Robert recruited new board members. Robert had watched as other nonprofits relied on board members to recruit other board members, but he believed that it was more advantageous for the ED to take that initiative and build relationships with potential board members in order to ensure the board and the ED were aligned.

Robert smiled as he thought of the seven board members he had recruited. These newest members shifted the dynamics of the board. One example was Melinda. Robert recruited Melinda, who worked at a local bank, to be the treasurer of the board. Melinda brought a fresh perspective, and she was supportive of Robert's efforts. Like other board newcomers, she told him, "If it were anyone else asking me to do this, I'd say no, but because it's you, and I want to help you turn this around, I'll come on board." While being supportive of Robert, it was her professional expertise that gave her credibility when she supported crucial initiatives, such as trying to increase transparency of funding decisions and making sure board members were not acting on matters that presented conflicts of interest. In shifting to a governing board, Robert ensured that fresh perspectives gave voice and urgency to tasks that had to be accomplished.

The next hurdle on Robert's list had been to determine how to ensure the providers CUEH funded were aligned with the expectations of the community and key stakeholders (i.e., police, hospitals, mental health facilities, etc.). To do this, he first had to capture stakeholder voices and determine what their expectations were and then communicate them to providers in such a way that they would make necessary changes at the system level. Indeed, he had seen over the last year that many of CUEH's providers were stuck in how they worked with the homeless population, particularly vis-à-vis what the community expected. For example, many of the providers had certain rules that they enacted when dealing with the homeless (e.g., putting them back on the streets if they did not stay on their medications) that did not always make sense to other stakeholders. These stakeholders expected providers to help people get off the street and struggled to understand why the providers would turn individuals away.

As he thought about this task, one example jumped to his mind. Robert thought of a woman who was sleeping in a high school vestibule during a particularly brutal cold snap. She had been kicked out of a housing project for not maintaining her mental health appointments. The police and members of the county government came to Robert saying, "This isn't right. What in the world, Robert? Why would they kick her out?" This situation represented just one of the many disconnects between the community (i.e., law enforcement, courts, local leaders, business leaders) and CUEH-funded providers.

It was situations like this that reaffirmed to Robert that he needed to help align the goals of providers and the community. Hearing these stories, Robert started challenging providers regarding their approach to the homeless population. Indeed, he had said in front of some groups, "Putting someone back into homelessness because they're not following your rules or they're not taking care of themselves the way you think they should be, I can't, I don't understand that, nor can I support it."

Besides making verbal arguments to providers to change their protocols, Robert also began to more fully utilize measurable outcomes to determine funding priority. Robert worked with community stakeholders to set the benchmarks to determine funding. Some providers struggled to accept this shift. Under the current system, the agencies receiving money and providing services were setting the standards. But Robert strongly believed in the value of having stakeholders inform the standards, as they knew the needs of the homeless population firsthand. In addition, Robert knew it was crucial to have consequences for not adhering to standards. So, in an effort to foster agency accountability and to increase the transparency of board decisions, CUEH started posting related information on their website, allowing anyone to see how providers were scoring on the variety of metrics used to evaluate providers. While this public display of results made many providers uncomfortable, Robert believed it was the best way to hold organizations accountable. These measures were, in turn, helping him enact systemic change in how providers engaged with the homeless and allowing CUEH to be consistent in determining funding priority.

The final task on Robert's list had been to mobilize a volunteer base in order to achieve his overarching goal—changing community views about homelessness. Robert wanted people to understand that homelessness was not a choice, but rather a symptom of other community issues (i.e., job loss, mental health, medical issues, family breakup, and domestic violence). Just as systemic-level changes were difficult, shifting beliefs about the homeless was equally challenging. Robert believed getting volunteers involved was central to help the community understand that homelessness was not a choice. Shifting beliefs about homelessness and mobilizing volunteers seemed like two separate goals to many, including some board members, but Robert believed they were intricately related as volunteers were able to both actively help the organization complete necessary tasks and spread the word to the larger community about not only the organization and its goals, but also the issues facing the homeless population. Therefore, Robert used a three-pronged approach to volunteers.

First, Robert tried to engage the homeless and formerly homeless in volunteer capacities. They had been on the front lines and understood the issues unlike anyone else. In this respect, Robert had reached out to previously homeless veterans to help with data collection. These veteran interviewers advised CUEH as to where to go to interview the homeless, how to interact with homeless veterans, and why the homeless might be reluctant to tell their stories. Similarly, CUEH was preparing for a "peer navigator project" in which they had enlisted five formerly homeless individuals to work in daytime centers and report back on what was working and not working in those centers.

This was similar to the approach Robert took when he worked with homeless youth. At that time, no one had believed there was such a thing as homeless youth. Rather, the youth chose to be homeless; they chose to leave home; and they chose to ignore the rules. Robert's response at that time was to find volunteers among the homeless youth—to get young people telling their stories to the community. Whenever he was speaking on the issue—whether to a local community group or to the state legislature—he took a youth volunteer with him to tell his/her story. And he saw results. Now, when encountering a homeless youth, people ask, "What did they grow up in?" Indeed, Robert and his volunteers managed to shift the paradigm by engaging those closest to the issue, and he was working to do the same at CUEH.

Next, Robert worked to utilize a traditional volunteer base and give them exposure to the homeless community. He recruited individuals to help with various surveys—a point-in-time survey mandated by the US Department of Housing and Urban Development and a vulnerability index. Each of these volunteer opportunities allowed individuals to engage with the homeless. Over the year, Robert saw people involved in that frontline effort become inspired, saying, "I'm going to go back to my school, my job, my church, wherever, and mobilize to help with this or that."

Robert had seen the impact of this mobilization before when working with the homeless youth. At that time, there was a high school junior who volunteered, and after doing so, she created a club at her school, engaging her peers in fundraising and volunteering. Robert was seeing the same thing happen currently as people were touched by stories they heard while volunteering.

Finally, Robert harnessed the power of unpaid interns. In his short time at CUEH, there had been half a dozen unpaid college interns, and he partnered with a college class to do a service learning project. Robert appreciated these opportunities to work with students because these "volunteers" had other commitments (i.e., to their university) and therefore were dedicated to having a final product, a product that was grounded in research. But, perhaps more importantly, Robert valued the process of involving students and getting them to look at an issue from various perspectives. It was an opportunity to impact how a person perceives the issue of homelessness for the rest of his/her life, and he knew from experience that those young people would be able to reach others with the all-important message that homelessness is not a choice.

KEY TERMS

Coercive Power - the ability to control others by taking away or withholding something they want or need.

Governing Board - a Board of Directors whose members focus primarily on leading the organization by developing a vision, setting policy, and providing financial oversight.

Reward Power - the ability to control others by giving them something that they want or need.

Working Board - a Board of Directors whose members work as unpaid staff for the organization in addition to fulfilling governance responsibilities.

DISCUSSION QUESTIONS

1. Leadership transitions are typically difficult for organizations. How might they be more complicated in organizations that rely on volunteers? How do we see this in Robert's account?

2. How does the leadership of this nonprofit organization (i.e., Board of Directors, executive director, staff, volunteers) differ from leadership of traditional for-profit organizations (i.e., president, CEO, managers)? In what ways can leadership of a nonprofit organization benefit from the leadership

style of for-profit organizations? In what ways can for-profit organizations benefit from the leadership style of a nonprofit organization?

3. What should be the roles and responsibilities of the Board of Directors? Do you agree with Robert's assessment that there needs to be a division of governance and operations? Do you agree with Robert's method of selecting the board members? Why or why not?

4. As organizations develop their Boards of Directors, what emphasis should be placed on experience in the field and connections in the community versus the ability to bring a fresh perspective?

5. From a communication perspective, how do nonprofit organizations ensure they are aligned with community initiatives? How might this be a reciprocal relationship?

6. In what ways did Robert utilize reward power? In what ways did he use coercive power?

7. Robert attempted to leverage volunteer resources for organizational change. What is the role of volunteers in enacting change?

8. In Robert's case, we see several voices enacted (i.e., CUEH, the Board of Directors, volunteers, community stakeholders). How might these voices further affect systemic changes? From a communicative perspective, what additional changes might these differing and sometimes conflicting voices consider?

SUGGESTED READINGS

Bisel, R. S., & Barge, J. K. (2011). Discursive positioning and planned change in organizations. *Human Relations, 64,* 257–283. doi:10.1177/0018726710375996

Lewis, L. K. (2007). An organizational stakeholder model of change implementation communication. *Communication Theory, 17,* 176–204. doi:10.1111/j.1468-2885.2007.00291.x

Seo, M., Putnam, L. L., & Bartunek, J. M. (2004). Dualities and tensions of planned organizational change. In M. S. Poole & A. H. Van de Ven (Eds.), *Handbook of organizational change and innovation* (pp. 73–107). New York, NY: Oxford University Press.

KEYWORDS

organizational change, reward power, coercive power, working board, governing board

---

*This case study is based on my yearlong affiliation with Counties United to End Homelessness. I have conducted observations in this organization, facilitated surveys of various organizational stakeholders, and my undergraduate class did a service learning project with this organization. This case study is grounded in what I have observed during these experiences, as well as a one-on-one 75-minute interview with the executive director.

CHAPTER THREE

Can THIS Collaboration BE Saved?*

JEANNETTE KINDRED AND CLAUDIA PETRESCU

Eastern Michigan University

South River Neighborhood Association (SRNA) and North River Economic Association (NREA) are both community development organizations located near each other in a large urban city in the United States. They have similar missions and serve the same diverse and largely low-income populations. Both organizations have been hard hit by the most recent recession, bringing in fewer grants and less money in fundraising.

SRNA is a grassroots organization, which has historically operated with an all-volunteer staff. After several years, SRNA was able to secure a renewable grant, which allowed them to hire a part-time executive director, Steve Rundell. Steve is 32 years old and holds a bachelor's degree in nonprofit management. Later, with similar funding, they hired a part-time staff member. SRNA's mission is focused on encouraging residential engagement in order to sustain a viable and safe community. They currently have a pool of over 80 long-term volunteers. Their services include preserving and building affordable housing, and protecting and beautifying the parks, waterways and recreational areas. With the decline in the economy and the recent loss of funding in grants and donations, however, the organization has been losing funds. The organization's budget dropped from $560,000 to $257,000 over a four-year period.

SRNA has been serving the community for over 40 years. Each of the 20 board members (all community members) has been committed to SRNA for several years. They are a working board—they organize events and are involved in providing services on a regular basis. The majority of them were long-term volunteers before joining the board. Presently, 12 of them have been on the board for more than 10 years.

NREA is a younger organization with a 15-year history in the community. They have three paid staff: a full-time executive director and two part-time employees. Their mission is to promote economic development by encouraging entrepreneurship and by providing support to businesses in the community. Their main services are to promote relocation of businesses, to revitalize the commercial district, and to provide business training. They have a pool of approximately 30–40 volunteers. The organization's budget has been stable for the last four years at about $425,000.

NREA has a different structure than SRNA. Their board consists of 12 members, each of whom serves a four-year term limit. They are considered a governance board, engaging in strategic planning and overall governance, but they do not engage in any hands-on activities of the organization. The board is economically diverse: two-thirds of the members are local residents, while the remaining members consist of a banker, a lawyer, a foundation officer, and a university professor. The executive director, Kamille Worth, has been in her position for more than five years. She is 36 years old and holds both bachelor's and master's degrees in urban planning.

For several years, these two organizations have coexisted and have worked together informally, as both are members of a larger community collaborative that consists of 12 community development corporations. The board members of each travel in the same circles and occasionally mention that it would be nice to create a more structured collaboration. Each, of course, has its own motive for doing so: SRNA would like to tap into the financial strength and business connections of NREA, while NREA would love to take advantage of the network of volunteers and building preservation and repair services offered by SRNA.

A Collaborative Grant Opportunity Arrives

A nonprofit capacity-building program grant was announced three years ago. The grant is funded by a local nonprofit management support organization, The Future of Nonprofit Organizations. The capacity-building grant is designed to help organizations develop and implement programs to build their capacity in two areas: organizational development and leadership. "I think we need to pursue this opportunity," the NREA board president said to his SRNA counterpart.

"I agree. It will be good for each of our organizations and for the community," replied the SRNA board president.

As part of the grant, the organizations selected to participate would receive a cash award of 15% of each organization's budget. To encourage collaborations in the community, the grant would also provide an extra $3500 support toward a joint collaborative project. Both organizations' board members agreed that this was the catalyst needed to finally work together.

The board presidents instructed their respective executive directors to work together on this grant. Steve and Kamille jointly wrote and submitted a proposal to create a comprehensive community revitalization program, which would include the development of a joint community marketing plan and a joint land and buildings use program. In mid-January, the two organizations were notified that they were accepted as a collaborative for the capacity-building program.

The Collaboration Timeline

February: Steve Rundell received news that a continuance of a grant that would have paid SRNA's staff salaries had been rejected. Steve did not see this coming. The foundation that rejected his application had been providing a grant to cover the SRNA salaries for more than a decade. Without having money to pay personnel expenses, the Board of Directors had no choice but to terminate Steve as well as the part-time staff person. As a result of this huge financial loss and with the need to keep the collaborative capacity-building grant moving forward, John Applegate, longtime board president and a retired autoworker, stepped down from the board and took on the role of unpaid interim executive director for SRNA. He is currently 63 years old and has been working regularly to build the community in which SRNA is located.

April: Both SRNA and NREA began the capacity-building program by completing a capacity-building self-assessment to determine their specific needs in the two areas of capacity building: organizational development and leadership. The funder mandated the self-assessment. Based on this assessment, the two were asked to develop a specific plan of action that would articulate how they would develop the collaboration to expand their joint capacity building. The grant required that the collaborative agencies together devise an action plan with specific goals and objectives that relate to the collaboration. The collaborative was given one year to create and implement the plan. By April 1 of the following year, they had to provide evidence that they were achieving collaborative goals. The funding organization's staff gave direction and guidelines as to creating this plan but left the process up to the two organizations and did not proactively intervene.

May–August: In late May, John moved to another state because of health issues. He did not want to give up his position as SRNA's interim executive director and still insisted on working with Kamille on the collaborative plan of action. However, he only communicated via phone or in person on the few times he came back to town. It was very difficult to get in contact with him, and although the two spoke on the phone, communication was infrequent. Kamille was excited and eager to move the process forward. She was open to phone calls and meetings, but she also made several attempts to communicate with John via e-mail. During this time frame, there was not much movement on completing an action plan. Also during this time, several back-and-forth phone calls occurred, between each executive director and the funding organization's staff, to complain that the other party was not cooperating.

September: John finally announced that he would come back to the state to work with Kamille on the action plan, but he insisted that he be paid from the grant as a "consultant." The funding organization's staff knew that the grant money could be used for consulting but only for those not affiliated with the organizations. The grant specifically could not pay salaries, and they explained to John that paying him as a consultant would be the same as paying a staff salary. His request was denied.

October: It was evident that John and Kamille were not regularly talking to each other, and the funding organization continued to encourage them to work together. There were, after all, only six months left in the grant's time frame. While other participants in the program were moving along nicely, building and executing their own plans, the SRNA–NREA collaborative was stuck. The funding organization was getting worried that there was no plan. The program was on a specific time frame, and the building of this collaborative plan was delayed due to lack of communication.

It was at this point that the funding organization decided to intervene and requested to meet individually with John and Kamille to discuss privately with each what had happened up until that point, what was currently going on, and how to proceed moving forward.

Meeting with John

During John's meeting, he expressed frustration with not only NREA staff, but with the funding organization's staff as well. "I don't think that NREA was really intent on collaborating with us," said John. "I don't think that either you or they see us as equals. They have staff, and we don't; they have a larger budget than we do. They act as if because of these reasons, they are better than us."

"On the few occasions that I talked to Kamille, she kept expressing concern about liability and kept asking to look at our financial statements. I was concerned by her requests, as was the rest of the SRNA board. We are not doing a merger with NREA; we are collaborating. I got the sense that when I refused to turn over our financials that there was not going to be a true collaboration."

"You know, they wanted all this information from us but were not very forthcoming on their own. Did you know that they are moving forward on collaborations with other community development organizations? I asked about it once and even suggested a joint application, but they never responded. If you want to work collaboratively, then you have to be more forthcoming."

At this point, John began to appear even more frustrated, this time with the funding organization's staff. "To be honest, even though your role is to be neutral, it has constantly felt as if you're on their side. When a board member or I call you with a concern, it feels as if you and NREA are ganging up on us. It's hard to work collaboratively when you don't feel as though you are an equally respected partner in the process."

John finished the meeting with this final statement: "Well, now that I think about it, even though we are similar kinds of organizations, we're really pretty different; so maybe the collaboration really wasn't a good idea to begin with. I'm not sure if or how we should go forward from here."

Meeting with Kamille

Kamille also expressed frustration with the collaboration process. "The process of course has been infuriating! John won't respond to any of my e-mails. I have sent him several plan drafts, but all he wants to do is wait and talk about the plan when he's in town. This is the 21st century; we can work electronically!"

"Personally, I think the staff changes at SRNA have a lot to do with the problems," Kamille continued. "Working with Steve on the grant proposal was relatively smooth, but then he was let go, and then their interim, John, leaves town. I naturally assumed that we would oversee the creation of the plan after this happened, since we are a more stable and properly structured organization. The plan drafts I sent list specific ways that we can support and oversee all aspects of the collaborative project. But everyone at SRNA seems to be on the defensive all the time. They really need to just admit that they are weak right now and need us to take the lead on this grant. We only want to help."

"One red flag, however, is that they seem to be hiding information from us. In order to work together, we have to understand where each other is financially, but John is really resisting sharing any information with us. My board is really starting to distrust SRNA; they have some major concerns about moving forward. We have actually reached out to other organizations to collaborate, just in case this doesn't work out."

Kamille added one final thought about the funding organization's staff: "You all have been so helpful. Anytime I called with concerns, I really felt supported and encouraged. I still have hope that we can make this collaborative work out."

After talking with John and Kamille, the funders shook their heads and wondered, what's next?

KEY TERMS

Capacity Building - actions that improve nonprofit effectiveness (Blumenthal, 2003).

Funder - a person or organization that provides money to support an organization's mission.

Governance - an operating system or theory of the board's role, position, practice, and relationships (Carver, 2006).

Nonprofit Collaboration - a mutually beneficial relationship entered into by two or more organizations to achieve common goals.

DISCUSSION QUESTIONS

1. How are the managerial and governance structures in each organization impacting the collaborative process?
2. What should the role of the funder be in a nonprofit collaboration? Should the funder have done something differently during the first six months of the grant? What should the funder do now?
3. What other stakeholders are potentially impacted by the problems with this collaboration (for example, board members or volunteers)? How should these stakeholders be included or informed during the process?
4. How do generational differences potentially create problems for collaborations between nonprofits?
5. What expectations and assumptions was each organization bringing into this situation? How did these assumptions impact the collaboration process?
6. Overall, can this collaboration be saved? What next steps should South River Neighborhood Association and North River Economic Association take?

SUGGESTED READINGS

Blumenthal, B. (2003). *Investing in capacity building: A guide to high impact approaches.* New York, NY: The Foundation Center.

Carver, J. (2006). *Boards that make a difference: A new design for leadership in nonprofit and public organizations.* San Francisco, CA: John Wiley & Sons.

Lewis, L., Isbell, M. G., & Koschmann, M. (2010). Collaborative tensions: Practitioners' experiences of interorganizational relationships. *Communication Monographs, 77,* 460–479. doi: 10.1080/03637751.2010.523605

Twenge, J. M., Campbell, W. K., & Freeman, E. C. (2012). Generational differences in young adults' life goals, concern for others, and civic orientation, 1966–2009. *Journal of Personality and Social Psychology, 102*, 1045–1062. doi: 10.1037/a0027408

Vlaar, P. W., Van den Bosch, F. A., & Volberda, H. W. (2006). Coping with problems of understanding in interorganizational relationships: Using formalization as a means to make sense. *Organization Studies, 27*, 1617–1638. doi: 10.1177/0170840606068338

KEYWORDS

collaboration, capacity building, community building, management

*This case study is loosely based on events that happened during a two-year capacity-building program in which the authors were directly involved. The federal government funded a $1 million grant and provided capacity-building support and assistance to several nonprofit organizations. Multiple sources of data were collected during the process, including survey and interview responses, as well as observational field notes and organizational documents.

CHAPTER FOUR

Splitting THE Baby

Collaborative Decision Making in Interpersonal and Organizational Crisis*

TIM HUFFMAN

Loyola Marymount University

Karen and Donna arrived at the youth house around 10:30 a.m. with a baby in tow. A client showing up with a baby was not unusual. StandUp For Kids was an outreach organization for homeless and at-risk young adults, and one of its services was running a drop-in center where youth under 24 could shower, do laundry, eat, access computers, and relax in a noninstitutional setting. Some of the homeless young women had children, and they often brought them. It was, however, odd that Karen and Donna came with a baby that day.

It was not their child.

Tim, the executive director, was told about the situation by his wife, Kristen. The baby, Devin, was Crystal's son, a young woman StandUp regularly served. Apparently Karen and Donna had babysat for the last few days, and Crystal was missing in action.

Later on the front porch, amid a group of youth and volunteers, Tim chatted with Karen and Donna.

"He won't sleep through the night," Karen complained.

"We actually got a noise complaint because of him crying because he has a fever," Donna added.

"Wow, that sucks," another volunteer replied. Tim nodded.

"I haven't been able to work on my homework. I'm missing sleep and not doing well in school," Donna went on. "We're supposed to have him until Monday, but it would be great if Crystal would pick up her phone. We know she turned it off because we've been calling her a bunch. He's got a fever, and he should go home." They tried to return the baby to Crystal but were confronted by staff at Crystal's apartment. When the apartment staff made a comment about Child Protective Services (CPS), Karen and Donna left.

At that point, Tim left to train new volunteers. As an all-volunteer organization, including Tim and the leadership team, volunteers fulfilled all sorts of tasks. They mentored and supported the youth, ran the drop-in center, went on outreach, coordinated efforts, and raised funds. Training took about 90 minutes.

After the training, Kristen pulled Tim and Sarah, another volunteer, into the office for an update. Apparently Karen and Donna called Crystal several times with no response. To make matters worse, they suspected she was on meth again. Finally, both Karen and Donna told Sarah that they had seen Crystal's boyfriend hit Devin in the face.

Tim had encountered various conflicts at StandUp before, but he had never had a possibly abused, possibly abandoned child show up at the center. Tim looked into the main room. Devin was huge for a nine-month-old, big enough to be two. He had light brown skin, adorably short hair, and smiled easily. Two of the youth were playing with him while Karen and Donna went to the store. As he laughed and played, Devin didn't look particularly neglected.

As they continued talking, Sarah felt very strongly that they should call CPS. Kristen was worried about the impact calling the authorities would have on the youth, including Karen and Donna. Kristen commented, "They asked us not to call CPS. They refer to CPS as 'Baby Jail.'" Karen herself had a daughter in foster care and had very negative experiences with it. Kristen, Sarah, and Tim discussed their options.

On one hand, CPS could be horrible as it could hook children into dangerous foster care. At StandUp, they were all too familiar with the foster system's limitations, since about 75% of their youth were in it at some point. On the other hand, Sarah pointed out that if StandUp knew a child was being abused, they should move forward because there was at least a chance the child would be treated better by a foster parent. If the worst was happening in Devin's home—violence, drug use, and abandonment—this was a pretty closed case.

At about that moment, Joey, another youth, stuck his head in and interrupted, "Does anyone know Karen or Donna's number?"

"No," Kristen said.

"Why?" Tim asked, almost holding his breath.

"Because Crystal is on the phone and wants to talk to them, but they aren't here."

It was go time.

"Can I talk to her?" Tim said, holding his hand out.

"Sure," Joey said and gave Tim the phone.

"Crystal! This is Tim."

"Hey, Tim," Crystal said in a totally normal, not drugged-out voice. "Have you seen Karen and Donna?"

"Yes, I have. They're around, but they went to the store."

"Well, dang. They have Devin, and my phone's broke. I need to talk to them."

"Actually, we have Devin," Tim replied.

"What?!?" Crystal said with surprise.

"They brought him here. We're looking after him right now," Tim explained.

"Oh my gosh, thank you," Crystal said with apparent relief.

This was Tim's chance to clear up some of the mystery. "Where are you?"

"I'm at my mom's," she responded.

"Karen and Donna said they've been trying to call you for a while, and you haven't answered."

"Well, that's because my phone broke! Someone dropped it in a pool, and I didn't have their number memorized. It wasn't until I thought of calling Joey that I had any way of contacting them," Crystal explained.

"Well, they've been pretty worried." Tim paused. His brain grasped for a kind and unalarming way to ask her about being on drugs. Nothing came to mind. "They're also concerned you've been doing meth."

"Meth?!? METH?!?! My phone broke! That's why I haven't answered. I didn't have their number because my phone broke!" Crystal said angrily.

"I'm not saying it didn't. I just had to ask." Satisfied with her indignant response, Tim moved to the next subject. "Can you come down to StandUp today?"

"I'm in Glendale at my mother's. I don't think so. Oh, no. My baby needs me. I can't get there," Crystal answered with a crackling voice.

His mind raced. "Lemme see what I can do. We might be able to send a volunteer to get you," Tim replied.

"Okay, thanks," Crystal said.

"I'll call you back in five minutes," said Tim.

"Thanks."

Tim walked back into the office. He laid out the situation of Crystal's seemingly total sobriety and the broken phone story. He thought that since there were no drugs and no abandonment, there was not much of an issue. He asked the others, "So, how much does this news change the situation?"

"Not at all," Sarah said emphatically. "There is, after all, still the issue of the boyfriend's domestic abuse." Kristen again highlighted a concern about calling CPS and how the other youth would react. "Devin and Crystal are well loved. We don't do ourselves any favors wronging them."

Tim made it clear that whatever they decided would have an impact, and that the youth would read the staff's reaction. It could also send a message that might prevent mothers from coming there in the future. Trust was a very important part of serving homeless young adults. If they didn't trust you, it didn't matter how many services you provided. Secretly, he was also thinking about how his decision would be read by other volunteers.

"Should we give the child back to Crystal?" Tim asked.

"How horrible will we feel if the kid gets killed while we think about reporting something?" asked Sarah.

Tim sensed tension in the room.

Sarah added, "CPS will take the call more seriously if StandUp has the child as opposed to some random call they get about a suspicion that they will take months to follow up on. But that's just what I think."

Trying to address the tension, Tim said, "I have no doubt that the people in this room will collectively make the right decision." The conversation continued, and they looked up the mandated reporting laws, since some occupations must report suspicions of child abuse. It made no mention of drop-in center staff, but counselors and social workers were listed. That was ambiguous and unhelpful, since at StandUp they were unpaid volunteers who often played the role of counselors and case managers.

The conversation turned to the fact that Devin may have bruises. Kristen suggested they check Devin, and they got him from the next room. Sarah played with him while investigating for any signs of abuse.

Kristen said, "I think it will be bad to have CPS pick the kid up from the youth house itself. That could be potentially flammable to our youth. We'd be violating Karen and Donna's request, and we may be seen as betraying Crystal. Some of the youth we serve have records or legal problems; we happen to think that shouldn't mean they starve. But bringing in law enforcement could drive off youth who have nowhere else to turn. But then, not reporting seems potentially immoral."

Tim asked if there were some middle ground. It was then that Joey stuck his head in. "Crystal is calling again."

"Thanks," Tim said, taking the phone. After Joey stepped out, Tim turned to the others, covered the phone with his hand, and spoke softly. "So, we aren't sending anyone to get her ..."

"No," asserted Sarah. "Tell her we don't have enough volunteers. It's her *kid*. If she really wanted him, she wouldn't need us to pick her up. She should have been here at 10 a.m. when the center opened because there was a possibility he would be here. She can walk from Glendale. She could crawl on her hands and knees from Glendale if it means picking up her kid."

When Tim broke the news that they couldn't come get her, Crystal broke into tears. "I can't believe this is happening. I can't make it down there by the time you close. I never should have left him. I never should have let him go."

"Crystal, we've got some concerns about your boyfriend. We've heard from different sources that he has been rough with Devin," confronted Tim.

Crystal responded immediately that her boyfriend loved Devin, that he did so much for him even though Devin wasn't his kid.

"My boyfriend isn't rough with my kid," Crystal asserted.

"Well, we heard Devin was hit in the face ..." Crystal broke down. She defended her boyfriend even more ardently.

"I wouldn't be with anyone who hurts my kid. I'm a good mother. I never go out anymore and always stay with Devin. I live my life for him," Crystal said emphatically.

"I don't think these accusations are true, but I feel obligated to take them seriously," Tim said. At the same time, though, Tim knew that Crystal's boyfriend was currently providing for her and keeping Devin and her off the streets. This financial dependence may have had her turning a blind eye.

Tim asked Crystal why someone might have the impression her boyfriend was abusive. She said sometimes her boyfriend played and messed with Devin, but not hard. Tim asked why the punching in the face might have been seen. "Maybe it's because I'm doing well. Maybe because I'm happy. Maybe some people are jealous. Maybe they want the old Crystal back. I have no idea." Eventually he calmed Crystal and told her he was not accusing her of being a bad mother, nor was he accusing her boyfriend.

"So, let me propose a course of action. Tell me what you think," Tim began.

"Okay," Crystal said reluctantly.

"I have a responsibility to report anytime I suspect child abuse," Tim began.

"Report to who?"

"CPS," Tim responded.

"CPS! Don't take my baby. I'll die for my baby! I'll kill for my baby! He's everything to me!" She began wailing. She said that they shouldn't call CPS, because she had CPS called on her when Devin was two months old. It had all gotten sorted out, and they had determined she was a good mother. She explained that the person who called CPS before was a terrible babysitter who didn't change his diaper and returned him with poop on his face.

Tim asked, "If someone were hurting Devin, wouldn't you want me to protect him? Wouldn't you want me to report something?"

"I wouldn't want you to report it. I'd want you to get that person put in jail and give Devin to me!" she exclaimed. Tim had a tough choice in front of him.

KEY TERMS

Group Decision Making - the communicative process of collectively identifying problems, positing solutions, and making choices.

Organizational Identification - the degree to which members of an organization see their identities as bound to the organization.

Organizational Identity - the distinct and identifying aspects of an organization, related to how the organization is perceived by others.

Voice - the expressed thoughts and feelings of groups or individuals. A particular person or group's voice can be augmented or muted, honored or manipulated, and attended to or dismissed.

DISCUSSION QUESTIONS

Group Decision Making

1. How should the staff make this decision?
2. Should Tim make an executive decision? Should they vote or continue discussing until consensus is found? Could all of the various concerns of the volunteers be met? If so, how?
3. In high-stakes, conflicted decisions like this, what do nonprofit leaders need to keep in mind?

Organizational Identity and Identification

4. What are the potential effects of involving a highly bureaucratic (and loathed by the youth) entity like CPS on StandUp's identity, a personal, nonbureaucratic organization designed to make youth feel welcome?
5. Could StandUp maintain its identity as being not part of the establishment? If so, how?
6. Are there ever times that a nonprofit organization should put aside its identity? Or should an organization's identity always be considered? Why or why not?
7. How might involving CPS impact identification with StandUp for volunteers and the youth they serve?

Voice

8. Did StandUp have an ethical obligation to speak on behalf of Devin?
9. To what extent should the consequences of breaking Karen and Donna's confidence regarding the alleged abuse (thereby using their voice in a

way they don't approve of) make a difference in what StandUp decides to do?

10. To what extent can nonprofits live up to the ethical obligation to speak whenever they see injustice but also respect confidences?

Organizational Policy

11. What policies could have been in place to assist with this situation?
12. Is it ever the case that lack of policies is actually a good thing? Why or why not?

SUGGESTED READINGS

Aust, P. (2004). Communicated values as indicators of organizational identity: A method for organizational assessment and its application in a case study. *Communication Studies, 55*, 515–534. doi: 10.1080/10510970409388636

Kuhn, T., & Poole, M. S. (2000). Do conflict management styles affect group decision making? *Human Communication Research, 26*, 558–590. doi: 10.1111/j.1468-2958.2000.tb00769.x

Mumby, D. K., & Stohl, C. (1996). Disciplining organizational communication studies. *Management Communication Quarterly, 10*, 50–72. doi: 10.1177/0893318996010001004

KEYWORDS

organizational identity, group decision making, voice

*This case study is drawn from a participatory action research project focused on compassionate communication and nonprofit organizations that served homeless youth. Findings from this project have been published in the *Journal of Social Justice*. This situation comes directly from field notes taken during the project.

CHAPTER FIVE

(Not) Fulfilling THE Promise

Susan G. Komen for the Cure in Crisis*

KRISTINA DRUMHELLER, EMILY S. KINSKY, AND
R. NICHOLAS GERLICH

West Texas A&M University

The big race day was less than nine months away as staff and volunteers of the local Susan G. Komen affiliate began discussing the latest turn of events from the parent organization. Susan G. Komen for the Cure, known for its pink ribbons and mission to cure breast cancer, had announced new funding strategies that excluded any organization that was under investigation. The new rule seemed to directly target Planned Parenthood.

Kary, a long-term volunteer with the affiliate, had been watching her Twitter feed for the better part of two days. Planned Parenthood tweeted the news early on January 31, "RT @ppact: ALERT: Susan G. Komen caves under anti-choice pressure, ends funding for breast cancer screenings @PP http://t.co/T17wWxHM." Kary herself had needed Planned Parenthood's services for her mammograms. One tweet hit close to home for Kary: "Planned Parenthood has been my primary provider of healthcare for HALF OF MY LIFE now. #PPSavedMe #StandWithPP." She didn't know where she would have gone for health screening if Planned Parenthood had not been available for her.

Although some supported Komen's decision, many people, including politicians and celebrities, were tweeting to pull support from Komen. Planned Parenthood tweeted, "JUST IN: Two dozen Senators #standwithPP, call on Komen to reverse Planned Parenthood decision: http://t.co/bIXZKl1B." Mayor Bloomberg chimed in: "Thank you to those standing with me in support of #PlannedParenthood. I'm matching contributions up to $250K. Join me http://t.co/JuWXu6mp."

Actress Aisha Tyler tweeted: "Women's health can't afford to be caught up in political bull. I #standwithPP. Do you? http://t.co/nWUlPKmX."

Kary worried about what the new decision would mean for her and others like her who relied on Planned Parenthood but loved the Komen organization. She was eager to visit with the affiliate director, Amy. As Kary walked into the offices, she could see staff and regular volunteers huddled around Amy. It was clear that everyone else was contemplating the same questions as Kary.

Kary overheard Cindy, the marketing director, say, "There is a lot of backlash against the grant-funding decision from cancer survivors. A friend of mine posted a video of a woman who had a mastectomy deriding Komen for politicizing breast cancer. I wonder how our volunteers, donors, and potential racers are taking the news?"

James, the volunteer coordinator, noted, "We've had nearly 400 e-mails in the last two days. Of those, 386 were against the new funding policy and only two were for it. I understand that some affiliates are on lockdown because of threats received."

"I'm glad we haven't received any threats," said Cindy, "but I'm still on edge. Clearly, there is a lot of passion surrounding this issue."

Amy added, "We have been getting calls from volunteers and donors since Tuesday's announcement. We've lost $50,000 from two of our corporate sponsors for Race for the Cure, and we could lose another three sponsors. This is really going to hurt us as the race approaches."

Amy and her staff continued to watch television, newspaper, and social media reports as supporters dropped Komen in favor of Planned Parenthood. Within 24 hours, Planned Parenthood had been given more than $650,000. Meanwhile, affiliates were withdrawing support. Amy read the Facebook posting of the Connecticut affiliate, "The decision regarding the funding of Planned Parenthood was made by Susan G. Komen for the Cure National Headquarters. Susan G. Komen for the Cure Connecticut enjoys a great partnership with Planned Parenthood and is currently funding Planned Parenthood of Southern New England. We understand, and share, in the frustration around this situation. We hope that any investigation prohibiting Planned Parenthood from receiving Komen grants is promptly resolved."

"They aren't the only affiliate disagreeing with Komen," said Cindy. "Affiliates in California are talking about taking a unified stand against the decision. Affiliates across the country are being hit as hard, or harder, than we are."

Amy was concerned about that as well. She knew the constituents in her area held generally favorable attitudes toward Planned Parenthood. Further, Amy knew Komen's managing director for community health programs had resigned in protest of the decision. This was not comforting news. As Amy contemplated the organization's next move, an audible groan was heard from Kary.

"This is going to make things worse!" said Kary. "Karen Handel just tweeted, 'Just like a pro-abortion group to turn a cancer orgs decision into a political bomb to throw. Cry me a freaking river.' Everyone knows Handel campaigned as a pro-life candidate for Georgia governor in 2010. This makes the entire decision look political, if it didn't before."

The staff nodded as Amy stated, "We need to decide what our response to the controversy is."

Taking a Stand

Although it was a difficult decision, all agreed that they were opposed to Komen's new funding policy. Through the affiliates' listserv, Amy learned of other directors willing to stand in solidarity against Komen's funding decision. She joined other state affiliate directors in sending notice to congressional leaders that they stood in opposition to Komen's grant-funding decision.

When Amy put on her suit the next morning, it felt as if she were putting on armor and war paint. The decision to oppose the parent organization was difficult. Amy felt a wave of fear and nausea, recognizing that she stood in opposition to a national policy and that she had no idea what would happen next.

Amy had personally visited with each of the corporate sponsors to gain their support of the local mission of the affiliate. She reminded them that while the Komen organization had a global reach, the local affiliate helped save lives in their home community. She pointed out that Komen's sponsors had allowed the organization to help thousands of women in need each year and to fund more breast cancer research than any other nonprofit organization—all without any government funding. Despite her passion, there were some sponsors who thought the association with Komen might tarnish their brand.

The Reversal

On February 3, Amy awoke to the news that Komen had altered its position. Komen released a statement that existing grants would continue to be funded and only those under *criminal* investigation would not be eligible to apply for funding. Komen CEO and founder, Nancy Brinker, had tweeted: "It's not about politics. It never has been and never will be. Get the straight story from me: [with http://t.co/MKME0pZg.[1]]." In her video apology, Brinker announced the changes in policy and apologized if anyone felt the decision had been made for political reasons.

Amy was afraid it would be difficult to recover from Komen's funding decision and reversal. The flip-flop was likely to affect giving from both those for and against the original decision. After assembling her team when she got to the office,

Amy stated, "We need to find out what kind of damage has been done. I'd like us to poll our community members to determine where they stand."

The staff put together a survey they posted on the affiliate Facebook site and e-mailed to volunteers. They asked that the survey be passed along to any willing participants. The results were disheartening. Amy wondered aloud, "How can things change so drastically and so quickly? How could pink ribbons go from being desired by everyone to being despised?"

Amy gathered her staff to discuss the findings. "The results indicate that we are likely to lose about 20% of our supporters. More than that, many who took the survey are being impacted by the social discussions about the controversy from their friends and social media."

Kary commented, "Social media responses have been favorably skewed toward Planned Parenthood. That can't be good for Komen or for the affiliates."

James agreed, saying, "We need to find a way to craft our message to win back our loyal supporters. Some of our relationships might be irrevocably damaged, no matter how much good Komen has done."

"We can't control what people are saying on social media, and the word spreads so quickly; how can we effectively respond to attract lost donors, racers, and volunteers?" asked Kary.

"I'm not sure," confided Amy. "Facebook and Twitter allow us to see opinions from everyone we have ever known. People aren't just relying on their close friends and family for public opinion. We are now being cheered and jeered by people around the world, from bystanders to stakeholders. This makes our messaging strategy all the more complex."

Amy knew that Komen clearly did not intend to create a firestorm with its funding decision. She still wasn't sure that politics hadn't played a part in the decision, but either way, people were disappointed. Amy was certain there was a way to improve how her local affiliate engaged with the public. She was eager to renew their faith in the organization's mission but didn't know where to start. She had to figure out how to appease volunteers, donors, racers, and other key members of her community.

Now What?

As autumn approached and race day grew closer, Amy wasn't sure what to expect. Washington, DC's affiliate race was down 25,000 racers. The New Jersey affiliate had lost $300,000 in donations in the course of nine months. Amy had been meeting with donors and sponsors regularly since February, trying to win back trust for her own affiliate.

"Our donors are still on the fence," said Amy, providing an update to her staff. "We have a lot of repairing to do. I don't know if the $50,000 in corporate sponsorship will come back, but we did manage to retain the other three sponsorships we almost lost."

Cindy noted, "It's a hard sell because it's a trust issue. It's going to take some time to undo the damage. It's not going to be easy with so many people shifting their donations from Komen to Planned Parenthood. I understand Planned Parenthood's donations are up, even though the decision was reversed after only three days."

James said, "If we can get back to the original focus and passion Nancy Brinker had when she founded Komen in 1982, we'll be okay. Her son, Eric, seems to think so, too. I was encouraged by his blog post that said, 'Most of the credit for the wealth of goodwill we've enjoyed over the years belongs to our local affiliates, on-the-ground volunteers, and generous corporate sponsors. We won't let them down again.' He also said they're making changes, including more board representation from local affiliates. According to Eric, although there have been some negative fundraising impacts in some areas, with Mother's Day races approaching, 'We're seeing our communities rally to help.' Maybe we'll be okay."

KEY TERMS

Crisis - an unexpected event that threatens the overall health and image of the organization. A crisis can be anything such as an act of nature, unforeseen accident, intentional misdeed, or terrorist act.

Image Reparation - an image restoration typology created by Benoit (1995) that was later changed to image reparation in recognition that organizations are more likely to repair, rather than restore, a damaged image from crisis. When an organization's reputation is threatened, the organization can engage in crisis response strategies to repair the reputation.

Organizational Image - the perception held by stakeholders, or key audiences, as shaped by the words and acts of the organization. Stakeholders can also influence the way the organization is perceived.

Theory of Planned Behavior - describes how individual intentions to engage in a behavior are an indicator of the likelihood of actually engaging in the behavior in the future. Intentions can be influenced by the individual's attitude toward the behavior, their perceived ability to control the behavior, and what their peers think about the behavior.

DISCUSSION QUESTIONS

1. What should nonprofit organizations consider when partnering with other nonprofit organizations? What should they consider when partnering with for-profit organizations?
2. How do you think Susan G. Komen for the Cure could have responded differently to this crisis?

3. What can Susan G. Komen for the Cure do to try to recover race participation as well as donations? What are its opportunities for renewal?
4. What ways can an organization repair its image with important stakeholders, especially when damaging situations might be out of their control, such
   as the case with affiliates of Susan G. Komen for the Cure?
5. What considerations do nonprofits have that for-profit corporations do
   not when engaging in crisis communication?
6. What role do you think our social peers play in decisions to give to charitable nonprofit organizations? In what ways do social media affect or
   influence peer groups?
7. How long do you think a person's plans to avoid donating to a nonprofit
   will last? Will these plans be permanent or short-term? Why or why not?

SUGGESTED READINGS

Benoit, W. L. (1995). *Accounts, excuses, and apologies: A theory of image restoration strategies.* Albany:
   University of New York Press.
Brinker, E. (2012, May 10). Mother's day in the mud. Komen Leadership News. [Web log.] Retrieved
   from http://blog.komen.org/?p=1038
Fussell Sisco, H. (2012). Nonprofit in crisis: An examination of the applicability of situa-
   tional crisis communication theory. *Journal of Public Relations Research, 24,* 1–17. doi:
   10.1080/1062726X.2011.582207
Kliff, S., & Sun, L. H. (2012, February 1). Planned Parenthood says Komen decision causes donation
   spike. *Washington Post:* Health & Science [online]. Retrieved from http://www.washingtonpost.
   com/national/health-science/planned-parenthood-says-komen-decision-causes-donation-
   spike/2012/02/01/gIQAGLsxiQ_story.html
Seeger, M. W., Sellnow, T. L., & Ulmer, R. R. (1998). Communication, organization, and crisis. In
   M. E. Roloff (Ed.), *Communication yearbook* (Vol. 21, pp. 221–237). Thousand Oaks, CA: Sage.
Shaw, D., Shiu, E., Hassan, L., Bekin, C., & Hogg, G. (2007). Intending to be ethical: An examination
   of consumer choice in sweatshop avoidance. *Advances in Consumer Research (ACR),* Orlando, FL.

KEYWORDS

crisis, nonprofit, Susan G. Komen, planned behavior, image reparation

*The affiliate organization in this case study is fictional and based partly on real affiliate stories. The
case is also based on research that appears in the *International Journal for Nonprofit and Voluntary Sector
Marketing,* the *Journal of Public Relations Research,* and a chapter in the book *Public Relations Theory
and Practice in the Nonprofit Sector.*

NOTE

1 Nancy Brinker's video apology and decision reversal was removed shortly after the controversy
   subsided in the media.

Staff Challenges: Stress, Ethics, AND Dissent

CHAPTER SIX

"I Don't Know Where MY Job Ends"

Workplace Stress and Social Support in Domestic Violence Prevention*

SUZY D'ENBEAU

Kent State University

ADRIANNE KUNKEL

University of Kansas

Susan pulled her car into the parking lot and took a deep breath. Today was her first official day as the new director of Harbor Safe House (HSH), a nonprofit domestic violence prevention organization that provided safe shelter, peer counseling, and other services to survivors of domestic violence across three counties. HSH consisted of 12 full-time staff members, three interns, and 10 volunteers. Susan had years of experience leading social work organizations, but she suspected that her tenure at HSH would be different. Susan opened the car door and turned on her smile as she hit the security buzzer and was let in through the door of the HSH center.

"Good morning!" Anna, her assistant, beamed. "I just updated your calendar. Let me know how I can help you prep for the board meeting tomorrow."

"Thanks, Anna," Susan replied as she made her way down the hallway to her office. She was facing pressures from all sides, and she knew the board would want answers, sooner rather than later. The board consisted of 13 members, who were each concerned about the future of HSH. During her final interview before getting the job offer, Susan was forewarned about the tensions between shelter and office staff that were exacerbated because of the different locations. Specifically, nine office staff members were housed in the main administrative building where Susan's office was also located. The remaining three staff members and volunteers worked in the shelter. Even though the shelter was only about 2 miles from the administrative office, staff and volunteers perceived that the distance was more like

100 miles! Susan was also alerted to the communication issues between management and subordinates and the need to secure more grant funding in an increasingly competitive environment. Susan wondered if these issues were causing the high staff turnover or if it was something else. She turned on her computer and prepared to tackle her to-do list.

In the office at the shelter house, Daria slumped into a chair at the conference table, where another advocate, Tanesha, was reading through a stack of survivor intake folders. Tanesha looked up to find Daria staring despondently at the stack of files.

"Is something wrong?" Tanesha asked.

"I've been having a difficult time with some of my clients. I'm working with a woman who calls me almost every day with long lists of needs like clothes and school supplies for her kids, assistance with paperwork for health benefits, and concerns about how she is going to pay her bills. I know we have a lot of resources available to assist survivors, but lately I feel like the downside of this assistance is that survivors think we can do everything for them. This particular survivor, who once stayed at the shelter, now lives over an hour away, and I've been driving back and forth to her house a few times a week, in addition to covering visits in my other areas. I haven't been getting home before nine o'clock every night, and then I'm here again at 8:30 each morning. I know I just earned my B.A. degree in social work six months ago, but my coursework didn't go over when and how to say no to clients. I just don't know where my job starts and where it ends. Everything feels like a crisis or an emergency, and my nerves are shot. It doesn't help that I can't talk to my boyfriend about all of this because of confidentiality."

Before Tanesha could respond, the crisis line rang. "I'll take this one," Tanesha said. Daria began to look through the intake files of survivors staying in the shelter while Tanesha talked with the caller. Daria couldn't believe they had processed six intakes last week and two new ones this week. She overheard Tanesha on the crisis line, and it sounded as if another survivor was going to come in that evening. That would make 30 total in the shelter, one of the highest occupancy rates HSH had experienced in months.

"You read my mind," Tanesha remarked to Daria as she hung up the receiver. "This shelter is getting fuller every day, and our volunteer advocate numbers are dwindling. They are the lowest I've seen in the three years I've been working here. In fact, shouldn't there be a volunteer here right now?" Just then, the office line rang. Daria picked up the receiver to hear Rose, a volunteer advocate, on the other end of the line.

"Hi, Rose. It's Daria. Please don't tell me you're calling to cancel your shift?" Daria halfheartedly joked with Rose.

"Yes, Daria," responded Rose. "Unfortunately, I do need to cancel my shift for later today. I thought I would be okay after last week, but I'm not. You remember what happened? Carol's abuser followed her here to the shelter, on her way home from work. He started pounding on the door, yelling profanities, and threatened to kill Carol if she didn't come out. I was the only advocate at the shelter, and I called the police. But it was a very traumatic experience. I don't feel like the volunteer training taught me how to respond to a situation like that. Honestly, I'm very frustrated that I was the only volunteer with a shift during that time, and to make matters worse, I couldn't get in contact with any staff members 'on call' to help me out. I need a bit more time to recoup before I pick up my shifts again."

"Thanks for letting us know, Rose," Daria replied. "I'll be sure to pass your message along to our new director, who said that supporting our volunteers is one of her top priorities. Please let us know when you would like to return. You are a wonderful volunteer." Daria hung up the receiver and looked at Tanesha.

"It sounds like Rose is not coming in tonight. We need to keep and take care of the volunteers we do have and recruit even more," Tanesha commented. "The volunteers complete a rigorous 40-hour training program and initially seem so motivated to work with us. But our volunteer retention rate is extremely low, and I think it might get worse given that we just lost another volunteer coordinator. That is the second coordinator to leave the position in less than six months. I thought Carin was doing a great job as the volunteer coordinator, but I guess Megan, the shelter manager, didn't agree. The last I saw of Carin, she was exiting Megan's office and wiping tears away from her face," Tanesha continued as she gathered up her purse and intake paperwork. "I hate to leave you to deal with the shelter on your own, Daria, but I have an appointment with a woman at The Sandwich Shop. She has been married to her husband for 10 years, and she is finally thinking about leaving. I am hopeful that I can help her get out of an awful situation." Daria wished Tanesha luck.

Tanesha arrived at The Sandwich Shop only to find it empty with a few employees laughing behind the counter. She ordered her sixth cup of coffee for the day, sat down at a table, and started to comb through the file of the woman she was supposed to meet. This woman had been beaten up for the fourth time that week, and the most recent time had sent her to the emergency room, where she was told that she might not regain full vision in her right eye. The woman had two small children, a four-year-old boy and a toddler who was only a year old. After reading through the file for a second time and finishing her cup of coffee, Tanesha decided the woman was not going to show up. She began to gather up her things, checked her phone, and saw that she had four missed messages from the shelter.

As she started listening to her messages, a young woman in her early 30s with a bandage over her right eye hurriedly opened the front door and frantically looked around. Tanesha gently raised her hand for the woman to notice. Reluctantly, the woman walked over to her.

"Please, sit down," Tanesha said in a calm voice. The woman nervously scanned the perimeter of The Sandwich Shop. After about 30 seconds, she sat down. Tanesha then asked her if she had started making formal plans to leave her abuser. Tanesha noticed that her unbandaged eye was welling up with tears as she said, "I gotta leave. But I'm scared. If I leave, Daniel is going to try to keep the kids. I know he will hurt them if I leave. And even if I leave, I know he will find me."

Tanesha listened to her story and put her hand on the woman's cold and trembling hand. Tanesha asked, "What can I do to help you prepare to leave? I have all kinds of resources to share with you, and we can even apply for some low-income housing in the area, though that probably won't come through for another three months. But it would be good to get the process started."

The woman replied, "I know I need to leave, but I'm not ready yet." With that, she jumped out of her chair and ran out the door, leaving Tanesha feeling as if she had failed.

When Tanesha returned to the shelter, she saw Daria on the phone and crumpled papers strewn everywhere in the shelter office. There was also a stench coming from the kitchen, possibly from a pile of dirty dishes or spoiling food. Knowing that she should begin to clean, Tanesha instead sat down in her chair and put her head in her arms. Daria ended her call and told Tanesha that she was about to leave to pick up another woman to bring her back to the shelter. As she prepared to walk out the door, Daria asked, "You okay?" After a long pause, Tanesha answered, "I just don't feel like I am doing my job very well. I try to help these women, but they don't accept the help. I try to talk to them, but I feel like everything I say is wrong. And this office is a total wreck, and I am too tired to do anything about it."

The crisis line rang. As Tanesha reached for the phone, she said, "Maybe if we could find a way to get the new director to come over here, we could show her that we are overworked and we lack the support to do our jobs." Tanesha waved to Daria as she walked out the door.

Later that evening, Susan let her mind wander while washing the dishes. Her husband, Bob, said, "You've had a long first day. Let me do that for you."

"Thanks for offering, but you know I find washing dishes to be therapeutic. I need to prioritize the different needs at HSH. The board wants me to focus on the big picture and not get bogged down with day-to-day issues. But we can't afford to have any more staff or volunteer turnover. Some staff and volunteers are clearly experiencing workplace stress and nearing the point of burnout. The work they do is important but also challenging, and the rewards are few and far between. How can I provide them with the support they need with the limited resources we have? I read an article that said talking about emotional stresses in your life can be therapeutic and healing. And I can see how this might be beneficial, yet we're constrained by rules of confidentiality. It's often the case that emotions fester and brew inside. No wonder so many employees and volunteers leave after only working there for a few months."

Bob put his arms around Susan's waist and replied, "I know you'll figure out the best way to approach the challenges at HSH. You always do." Bob kissed Susan on the cheek. Susan finished putting the last dirty dish in the dish rack, turned the light out in the kitchen, and retired to the family room. She wondered if she would be able to focus on anything else besides her work. Could she turn it off?

KEY TERMS

Social Support - the activity of caring, comprising messages and behaviors that provide assistance and comfort to distressed others.

Workplace Stress - cognitive or emotional experiences of overload or inadequacy to cope with professional obligations and duties.

DISCUSSION QUESTIONS

Workplace Stress

1. What are the main sources of workplace stress experienced by the different characters?
2. Why did Tanesha feel as if she "failed" with the woman at The Sandwich Shop? What would it look like if she succeeded?
3. What kind of strategies would you recommend to nonprofit staff and volunteers to avoid workplace stress? How can they learn to "turn it off" when they are not at work?

Social Support

4. What kind of training and support should HSH provide for volunteers, like Rose, so they are better prepared to handle difficult situations? What kind of training and support should staff receive?
5. How can nonprofit staff, like Tanesha and Daria, provide social support to their clients and also to one another?

General Stress and Social Support in Nonprofit Organizations

6. How much of a role should management play in providing support to nonprofit organization staff and volunteers? What should that role look like?
7. How can volunteers be recruited (and rewarded) to work at nonprofit organizations that require working in stressful conditions?

8. How can nonprofit staff and volunteers have a safe context to talk about their feelings when they are explicitly told to not talk about any of the work or clients because of issues of confidentiality?

SUGGESTED READINGS

Ashcraft, K. L., & Kedrowicz, A. (2002). Self-direction or social support? Nonprofit empowerment and the tacit employment contract of organizational communication studies. *Communication Monographs, 69*, 88–110. doi: 10.1080/03637750216538

D'Enbeau, S., & Kunkel, A. (2013). (Mis)managed empowerment: Exploring paradoxes of practice in domestic violence prevention. *Journal of Applied Communication Research, 41*, 141–159. doi: 10.1080/00909882.2013.770903

Myers, K. K., Seibold, D. R., & Park, H. S. (2011). Interpersonal communication in the workplace. In M. L. Knapp & J. A. Daly (Eds.), *Handbook of interpersonal communication* (4th ed., pp. 527–562). Los Angeles, CA: Sage.

Pennebaker, J. W. (1997). *Opening up: The healing power of expressing emotions* (rev. ed.). New York, NY: Guilford.

KEYWORDS

domestic violence, workplace stress, social support, volunteers

*This case study is based on ethnographic research conducted at a domestic violence prevention organization that resulted in publications in *JACR* and *Communication Currents*. The analysis that informs this situation comes from interviews with staff and volunteers who were experiencing role confusion, stress, and burnout. Staff and volunteers were looking for ways to effectively support one another while also empowering survivors of domestic violence.

CHAPTER SEVEN

Stress AND Burnout IN A Small Nonprofit Organization*

TAMAR GINOSSAR

University of New Mexico

JOHN OETZEL

University of Waikato

It was Saturday morning. Lisa rolled out of bed early, quietly, so as not to wake up her husband. She was tired but had to sneak into the office where she worked to get some things done. Coffee would have helped her feel more energetic, but the coffee jar had been empty for days. She would get her coffee at the office. They always had coffee and cookies to share with clients. It was no breakfast of champions, but she promised herself to get something healthier for lunch.

She felt guilty about going to work on a weekend and not being with her husband, but she had no choice. She worked for a small nonprofit organization (NPO) with a small team. They received funding from different sources, including their state, and were never secured in their funding to hire the number of people needed to complete the work. When she had left the office late the night before, there was a tall pile of forms on her desk. There was a pile of forms on every desk in the office, and, in fact, forms seemed to cover every space in the small, crowded agency that was a converted doughnut shop. She knew her husband would be disappointed when he woke up and discovered that she was gone again. What he did not understand was that each form represented a person. If not filled in correctly and sent on time, these people would lose their food stamps, the medications that kept them healthy, their access to medical care, and even their homes.

The weekends were the only days when she could catch up, when no new clients would walk in in complete despair after being diagnosed or because their electricity was disconnected or simply because they wanted to talk to someone.

It would be only she and the forms, and she would fill out all of them, except for the medical information, of course. She had to wait and call the clinic on Monday, hoping that the experienced nurse would be there and would have time to answer all her questions, but she would worry about that on Monday.

For the time being, she would take her dog, Toto, to the office; the poor puppy had not gotten a good walk for days and taking him made her feel safe. She still remembered the time when she'd arrived at work on a Monday morning and discovered hateful graffiti sprayed on the walls over the weekend. It was not easy to provide services for HIV positive clients in a small town. There was no sign on the office door and no indication of the diagnosis that their clients shared, but you could not keep secrets in a small town. Although they immediately painted over the graffiti, it was hard to forget the incident that made all of them look over their shoulders. Luckily, only a few clients knew about the graffiti. Many clients were already concerned about stigma and discrimination, and their stress always affected her.

She was well into her second form when Toto growled. The doorknob turned, and the door opened. Lisa's voice cracked a little: "Who is it?" and her dog lunged at the people in the doorway. She should have known. It was Natasha, the agency's director. Natasha looked just as startled as Lisa. Her black hair, always well combed, was now tied in a ponytail, and her face was clean of makeup. She held her little boy's hand in one hand and a pile of children's DVDs in the other. As the dog leaped happily to great them, she dropped the pile and the discs fell, making a loud sound. "I'm sorry. I thought no one would be here!" both of them exclaimed at the same time and then laughed.

Three hours later, they were still working. Lisa's dog was curled next to her, and Natasha's son was watching his second animated movie. It was time for lunch. The smells from the nearby diner were tempting, but Lisa knew she could not afford to buy lunch. Payday was still a few days away, and her budget was tight. Luckily, they had ramen noodles in the kitchenette. It was a nice break, as the three of them sat and talked.

Lisa always cherished the rare private moments with Natasha. She secretly admired Natasha, who was just a few years older but had a unique inner strength and was the backbone of their agency. She knew how to hire good people, how to train them, and how to support them. Equally important, she had mastered the art of working with the different state and federal agencies, securing grants, and navigating the complicated terrain of paperwork and incredible bureaucratic hurdles and regulations. She not only kept the agency afloat during difficult times; she also managed to grow it.

The minute Lisa walked into the agency a year earlier, she had felt an instant connection. The small space was bursting at the seams with 10 staff members and a constant stream of clients. It had a warm, busy atmosphere, and it immediately felt like home. During her interview, Natasha asked her if she had previous experience working with people living with HIV. Lisa had to admit that she did not. Having to cope with a constant state of crisis in her own family had made her strong, caring, and interested in working with people in need. She also learned not to judge people, as her family dealt with different challenges, but she did not know anyone who had HIV. She could hardly believe it when Natasha called her the next day to tell her that she got the job. She later learned that Natasha and the team were hiring people based on their empathy and personality. "You can always learn about HIV, but you cannot learn to have empathy!" Natasha always said. She was right, as usual.

Lisa had spent the last year learning about HIV. She learned from her co-workers and in training that Natasha carefully selected. Some workshops were for "newbies" like Lisa. For others, the whole team would go. Natasha would leave one person in the office "to hold down the fort," and the others would cram into a minivan and drive. There was no training in their town, and out-of-town training was expensive, but Natasha somehow managed to find funding for them. It made Lisa feel professional, and she knew from the regional meetings that her team was just as knowledgeable, if not more so, than case managers working in the city.

Certainly, her team seemed to get along better than other teams. Maybe it was the nights sharing a motel room with three colleagues or the long drives in the old minivan with the broken radio. Maybe it was the coffee and cookies, but her work environment felt like a second family to her. She knew she could count on her coworkers and Natasha. When she had to take time off to be with her ailing mother, she knew the other case managers would take good care of "her" clients, and Natasha told her to take as much time off as she needed. Whenever there was an important decision to make, they were all involved in making it, and they celebrated together in good times and bad.

Her intuition when she'd walked into the agency that first day was correct. She loved her job. It was much more meaningful and satisfying than working in a corporate environment, as did many of her childhood friends. Although she did not earn as much at this nonprofit agency as they did, she felt that she made a difference. Sure, her clients were sometimes challenging. Some of them went through bouts of bad moods, and it was particularly difficult to see those few who seemed unable to make good choices about their medical care, but Natasha helped her to keep all of this in perspective. "We are a family. We might have some disagreements with our clients, like any family, but they always know that we care about them and that they can count on us." Natasha was right, and Lisa had some great moments seeing people turning their lives around.

She also learned from her clients. Ervin told her about the days in which contracting HIV/AIDS resulted in a painful death. "I left town and moved to San Francisco in the early 90s. Many of my best friends were dying. There was no cure. When I was diagnosed, I came home to die. But then I was one of the first people in the country to receive the new effective AIDS treatment, and I am still here today." Listening to these stories, Lisa could not help but think how difficult it must have been to work with people with HIV back then. She was so lucky to live in this day and age, so lucky to have her job, her clients, her coworkers ... So why was she feeling so down? Why was she so emotionally exhausted and tired all the time lately?

The other day, she caught herself being very short with a client. The woman was telling her about her children and her bills while Lisa was trying to input all the necessary data when the computer crashed. It was her third time trying to enter the data. Every time the software would "freeze," and all the information was lost. Then her client complained that she was not looking at her. "How can I look at you when I need to enter the data? Can't you understand that I cannot help you unless I enter this information?" The poor woman was taken aback by Lisa's anger. She did not say another word, and when she left, Lisa felt guilty. Many clients had very difficult lives, and she was there to help and support them, not to be a source of stress as they tried to understand how to navigate the system. However, it was increasingly difficult to remember this when the computers kept freezing up and the paperwork kept piling up on her desk.

Natasha must have read her mind. "Lisa, I noticed you're very stressed lately. Is everything okay at home?"

Lisa felt a sudden rush of anger. "Home? I wouldn't know if everything is well at home. I'm barely there!"

Now it was Natasha who was taken aback by her response. She sighed before she answered. "Our workload seems to have increased lately. We always had to reenroll clients every six months and to help them fill in these complicated forms, which they cannot always understand, and at times neither can we. But with all the new regulations and funding cuts, it's been more difficult lately. I heard that half the case managers at the agency in the city left. This is a big turnover, even for them."

Her words made Lisa feel better. "I like working with clients. It's very rewarding to make a difference. And," Lisa continued, "I like working with you and the team. We are really like a family. I don't even care about the small paycheck I bring home. It's all worth it. But I feel that the 'higher-ups' only care about the forms, not the people behind them. Our work with people is now reduced to filling out forms correctly, and we have a computer system that is terribly slow and cumbersome. Fortunately, we have a great team—if we didn't have each other, I'd probably have left like those folks in the big agency. I talked with one of them at the last training, and he told me about how miserable it was working with his colleagues. Everybody is nasty to each other, they don't work together, and their supervisor makes all the decisions without any team input. Coupled with that, their employees have three times our case load. No wonder they lost half their staff. They might have better Internet connections than we do, but not the personal connection we have with each other and with our clients! Still, I'd rather be spending the weekend with my husband, and I never seem to have enough time to do my job. I'm so frustrated."

"Lisa," Natasha asked quietly, "do you think you are burned out?"

KEY TERMS

Burnout - a psychological syndrome that is caused by experiencing chronic occupational stress resulting in emotional exhaustion, reduced professional accomplishment, and demonstrated callousness toward service recipients and peers.

Organizational Culture - a set of practices, beliefs, assumptions, and ways of interacting shared by members of an organization.

Organizational Identification - the degree to which a person's sense of self is related to his or her workplace membership.

Social Support - the degree to which a person perceives and has the experience of being connected to social networks, being cared for, and having access to emotional, tangible, informational, and relationship resources.

Stress - an individual's experience of mental, physical, or emotional strain in response to a demand that the individual perceives as challenging. Chronic work-related stress might lead to burnout.

DISCUSSION QUESTIONS

1. In what way does Lisa's identification with her organization play a role in her experiencing stress? Can such identification increase burnout or prevent it? Please explain.
2. What might nonprofit employees do if they think they are becoming burned out?
3. What might nonprofit executive directors do if they suspect stress and burnout among their staff?
4. Comparing the organizational culture in the NPO in the small town with that in the big city, what factors might increase employees' stress?
5. Can or should NPOs have a policy to protect employees from burnout? If so, what procedures would you implement for such a policy? What kinds of social support might the NPO offer/provide for employees?
6. Do NPOs' employees differ in susceptibility to burnout compared with employees working in for-profit organizations? Why or why not?

SUGGESTED READINGS

Ginossar, T., Oetzel, J., Hill, R., Avila M., Archiopoli, A., & Wilcox, B. (In press). HIV healthcare providers' burnout: Can organizational culture make a difference? *Aids Care*.

Lewis, D. (2003). NGOs, organizational culture, and institutional sustainability. *Annals of the American Academy of Political and Social Science, 590*, 212–226. doi: 10.1177/0002716203256904

Maslach, C. (2003). Job burnout: New directions in research and intervention. *Current Directions in Psychological Science, 12*(5), 189–192. doi: 10.1111/1467-8721.01258

Maslach, C. (1976). Burned-out. *Human Behavior, 5*(9), 16–22.

Maslach, C., & Gomes, M. E. (2006). Overcoming burnout. In R. MacNair (Ed.), *Working for peace: A handbook of practical psychology and other tools* (pp. 43–49). Atascadero, CA: Impact Publishers.

Miller, K. I., Stiff, J. B., & Ellis, B. H. (1988). Communication and empathy as precursors to burnout among human service workers. *Communication Monographs, 55*, 250–265. doi: 10.1080/03637758809376171

KEYWORDS

burnout, nonprofit organization, organizational identification, organizational stress, social support

*This case study is based on a statewide community-based research project that aimed at assessing HIV services in federally funded agencies in a southwestern state. Data collection included interviews and focus groups with diverse clients and providers, including case managers and administrators in urban and rural NPOs.

CHAPTER EIGHT

Challenges IN Volunteer Management

Does It Really Have to Be This Hard?*

BRITTANY L. PETERSON
Ohio University

LACY G. MCNAMEE
Baylor University

It was a sunny fall afternoon as Caleb finished setting up his booth for the annual service fair. With more than a dozen other community organizations on campus that day, he tried his best to make the Child Watchdogs booth stand out with glossy information pamphlets, pens, lanyards, notepads, and, of course, candy.

"Okay, all set with a few minutes to spare," Caleb thought.

Out of habit, he unlocked his phone and browsed the inbox. Scrolling through, he stopped at a message from one of his newest volunteers and groaned. Erika's one-word subject line, "Resignation," said it all.

"Geez, only three weeks since training ended," Caleb thought despairingly. That class started with 15 new recruits, his biggest group yet, and Erika seemed so excited at orientation. That class had also reenergized Caleb, but this news rekindled the confusion and frustration that had crept into his life at work in recent months.

Since taking on the volunteer recruiter role at Child Watchdogs, Caleb had managed to nearly double the number of new volunteers in each training class—something he credited in large part to *finally* getting the new promotional materials he proudly displayed on the table. His favorite new pamphlets featured a volunteer with arms spread wide, anticipating a hug from the smiling child running toward her. Caleb remembered specifically choosing them because they captured the "feel good" emotions and experiences that came with being a Child Watchdogs volunteer, a message that seemed to really work at getting prospective volunteers through the doors. Nonetheless, something was obviously still broken. Yes, recruits were pouring in, but, like Erika, many didn't last.

Lost in his thoughts, Caleb pondered what was causing the revolving door of volunteers—and, more importantly, how it could be stopped. From what he could tell, a lot of dropouts were leaving for other volunteer opportunities that seemed more "fun" or "stress-free." Over the past few months, he had begun to question whether people were running for the hills as soon as things got "real"—that is, when they discovered all the difficulties of working with abused and neglected children. He scanned through Erika's e-mail again:

> *Hey Caleb,*
>
> *I'm sorry to do this, but I've been thinking … I just don't think I'm cut out for this. The kids are great … it's just … I'm in over my head. I just don't feel comfortable in the kids' homes, dealing with the parents. I never know what to say. Last week, one mom just about brought me to tears. I guess I just didn't think it would be this hard.*
>
> *Thanks for understanding,*
> *Erika*

Erika's excuse for leaving confirmed his suspicions, pushing him further into an anxious trance.

"Hellooo … earth to Caleb," said Sarah jokingly, waving her hands between Caleb's blank stare and his phone. "Look! My booth's right next to yours." Snapping out of his trance, Caleb gave the Teen Ministry volunteer coordinator a halfhearted grin but then thrust his phone in her direction.

"Check it out. It's happened again," he grumbled. Startled, Sarah took his phone and read through the e-mail, but before she could respond, Caleb quipped, "All my volunteer training efforts down the drain." After a few moments of tense silence, he added, "You know what, Sarah? Today my presentation's going to be different than in years past. I'm going to tell prospective volunteers how it *really* is working with the kids. I'm going to give them a true sense of the volunteer role … the real preview, no more surprises." Sarah nodded empathetically, knowing Caleb's frustrations.

"I'm so sorry, Caleb," she said. "Some days, our job is just plain tough. It's like darned if you do, darned if you don't. One of the hardest things for me is trying to figure out how to attract new volunteers—letting them know the good, the bad, and the ugly—without losing them right off the bat. Right now I feel like I'm constantly dealing with the ugly." She sighed and began venting to Caleb about her latest volunteer drama. Just last week she had sat in an empty classroom on campus wondering whether or not any of her volunteers were going to show up for the emergency meeting she had called.

"A teenager that one volunteer mentored had just been admitted to the hospital after a car crash. Alcohol was a factor, and I felt like I needed to debrief my volunteers before they heard the story elsewhere, you know." Sarah went on, "Caleb, I'm telling you, I sat in that room silently willing those students to walk through the door. And you know how many did? THREE."

"Out of how many?" Caleb questioned.

"Twenty! Can you believe that?! Apparently, only three of my volunteers are *actually* invested in Teen Ministry and in these kids' lives," Sarah moaned. "I just don't know how to make them care."

Sensing they needed to "get it together" before students arrived, Sarah turned back to her table and aimlessly rearranged items. In the silence, Caleb mentally revised his presentation, thinking about how he would use his five minutes onstage for each organization to speak.

Meanwhile, Sarah quietly reflected on her supervisory style and considered whether it really worked for her volunteers. She tried so hard to train her volunteers well and equip them for all the scenarios they might encounter when working with troubled teens. Some days, she left meetings feeling triumphant. After a recent session when one volunteer expressed frustration about feeling "micromanaged," Sarah explained that she wasn't trying to breathe down her neck, that she just needed to be kept in the loop with what was happening so that she could help. It felt good to clear that up and get everyone on the same page.

Still, more often than not, Sarah felt as if volunteers tuned her out. During meetings, she could see them texting, e-mailing, whispering to one another as she spoke. Sure, volunteers showed up for the "Connection" sessions to see their teens, but they often skipped team meetings and ignored rules designed to keep them safe. Just last week, Sarah heard that one of her volunteers was repeatedly driving teenagers around, even though they weren't supposed to have them alone in their cars.

A crackling microphone snapped Sarah back to reality. As she watched students flood into the courtyard, she said to Caleb, "You know, I think what I need to do is to inspire passion in the volunteers. I need them to see just how awesome it is to devote their lives to serving these teens. Give them a true sense of community—like they're part of a family. If they're 150% committed to the cause and to one another, I just know things will flow more smoothly."

"I'm with you," Caleb replied. "Here goes nothing!"

With that, the two of them turned their attention to the line of students forming in front of them.

Thirty minutes later, Sarah called toward Caleb, "You ready?"

"Yep," Caleb replied. With the open house portion of the service fair over, the recruitment presentations were about to begin. Sarah and Caleb walked side by side toward the staging area as students found their way to the folding chairs on the courtyard lawn.

"So many fresh faces," Caleb commented.

"Hopefully some of them will actually sign up!" joked Sarah.

"Well," said Caleb, "Ready or not, here we go."

****

As Caleb was taking the stage, Joy took a seat in the back next to her friend Sophia. Rushing from another on-campus meeting, she was late to the service fair but managed to grab pamphlets from each organization's table before she sat down. Joy settled in, leaned over, and whispered cynically in Sophia's ear, "*Obviously*, everyone's here to save the world."

"Ha. Yeah, just a bunch of 'do-gooders' trying to make the world a better place." Sophia smiled, sarcastically referring to students who were simply trying to get the 30 hours of volunteer service required for their degrees or the overachievers searching for yet another line on their résumés.

Joy laughed aloud. "Shhh! You're going to get us in trouble," she teased. "I am really interested in this one, actually," Joy said, pointing to the Child Watchdogs pamphlet and Caleb onstage.

Looking at the volunteer and child on the cover of the Child Watchdogs brochure, Joy thought, "Cool, I would love to work with kids." But when Caleb started talking about what it was like to volunteer, her attitude quickly changed.

"What?! Who wants to be in a situation where parents might wave a gun in your face? Or where you have to go to a house in the middle of nowhere where your cell phone doesn't work?" Joy thought. By the end of Caleb's presentation, Joy had decided there was no way she would volunteer for them. No way whatsoever.

"Hey, I think Teen Ministry might be cool," Sophia whispered to Joy as Sarah took the microphone next. "We could do it together, too, and I bet it won't drain you as much as it sounds like Child Watchdogs would." Onstage, Sarah excitedly began her speech.

"Teen Ministry is a way of life. It's a passion. A calling," she said. Sarah continued, sketching out the guidelines and requirements. "To make a serious impact, you make a serious commitment. For instance, volunteers sign a formal contract that commits them to the organization for at least one year. There are biweekly meetings and mandatory team-building sessions. Your team is your life—you're 150% committed to them, and you can rely on them no matter what. It's like your family."

"Well, that's kind of intense," thought Sophia after hearing Sarah speak. She appreciated the idea of teamwork, and she could see how being connected with other volunteers could be important. Still, she wondered if she had the time to get that invested in anything other than her studies.

Joy was also on the fence. "Hey, you know me," she whispered to Sophia. "I can handle commitment and having a lot on my plate. But all that talk of the 'team support' makes me wonder if you can even make a decision on your own."

"Yeah." Sophia nodded in agreement. "And there's a difference between being supportive and being buddies. I mean, I have enough friends. I feel bad saying that … but it's true. I just want to make a difference and do some good. I don't need a new social circle. Even if I have time for it … I just don't know if I want all that."

****

"Hey, how do you think it went?" Sarah asked Caleb after the presentations as they headed back to pack up their tables.

"I don't know," Caleb answered. "Hopefully telling them about all the challenges of being a Child Watchdog on the front end will cut down on the turnover I'm dealing with. Still, I wonder if I shared too much …"

Sarah shook her head. "Sometimes I feel like we just can't win. I tried to get people excited, but I'm afraid I might have scared a few of them off, too."

"There's always next year," Caleb kidded. "Besides, if you weren't always struggling to keep your volunteers, you wouldn't get to hang out with a great guy like me!"

Sarah laughed and smiled at Caleb, but as she turned away to head back to the office, she thought, "Does it really have to be this hard?"

KEY TERMS

Complementary Dialectics - reenvisioning dialectical tensions as capable of being synthesized, reframed, and collectively embraced.

Organizational Dialectics - ever-present, oppositional tensions that are part of organizational life.

Realistic Recruitment - in contrast to traditional recruitment practices, realistic recruitment entails conveying some negative aspects of an organizational role to prospective members to enhance member commitment and retention.

Third Membership Contract - volunteer membership is often characterized as a "third contract" that is distinct from employment-based membership and family/social affiliations.

DISCUSSION QUESTIONS

Organizational Dialectics

1. Nonprofit organizations often struggle with the dialectical tensions in volunteer management of *attracting* but also *adjusting* volunteers to their roles, providing them individual *ownership* but also supervisory *oversight*,

flexibility but also *formalized* standards and expectations, and fostering *intimacy* but also respecting and giving them *distance* in their relationships with fellow members. Identify these four dialectical tensions in the case. What are the difficulties in managing these dialectics, both as the NPO and the volunteer?

2. To what extent would these dialectics still apply in situations where volunteers didn't have as extensive responsibilities and commitments? How does organizational context play a role in how these dialectics are experienced?

Volunteering as a Third Membership Contract

3. In what ways are the expectations for volunteer membership different from that of traditional employment?

4. In light of this, what should managers consider when setting expectations for volunteer commitment, performance, and relationships with other members?

Volunteer Recruitment and Retention

5. To what extent did the managers in the case communicate realistic recruitment practices?

6. How might nonprofit leaders conduct recruiting and training sessions in ways that attract prospective volunteers but also realistically prepare them for their roles?

7. In nonprofit organizations, managers often have to find a balance between establishing rigid guidelines to protect their volunteers and knowing when to bend the rules. As a volunteer manager, in what instances would you enforce the rules? Bend them?

8. How can managers balance the tension between being too "hands-off" and too "overbearing"? What are the implications of giving volunteers too much freedom in their roles? Too little freedom?

9. To what extent should volunteer managers try to foster a family-like atmosphere? What are the strengths and weaknesses to adopting an approach where volunteers are expected to be "all in"?

SUGGESTED READINGS

Ashcraft, K. L., & Kedrowicz, A. (2002). Self-direction or social support? Nonprofit empowerment and the tacit employment contract of organizational communication studies. *Communication Monographs, 69*, 88–110. doi: 10.1080/03637750216538

Ganesh, S., & McAllum, K. (2012). Volunteering and professionalization: Trends in tension? *Management Communication Quarterly, 26*, 152–158. doi: 10.1177/0893318911423762

Kramer, M. W. (2011). Toward a communication model for the socialization of voluntary members. *Communication Monographs, 78,* 233–255. doi. 10.1080/03637751.2011.564640

McNamee, L., & Peterson, B. (2014). Reconciling "third space/place": Toward a complementary dialectical understanding of volunteer management. *Management Communication Quarterly, 28,* 214–243. doi: 10.1177/0893318914525472

Modaff, D., Butler, J., & DeWine, S. (2012). Realistic recruitment. In *Organizational communication: Foundations, challenges, and misunderstandings* (pp. 131–145). New York, NY: Allyn & Bacon.

Tracy, S. J. (2004). Dialectic, contradiction, or double bind? Analyzing and theorizing employee reactions to organizational tension. *Journal of Applied Communication Research, 32,* 119–146. doi: 10.1080/0090988042000210025

KEYWORDS

organizational dialectics, volunteer management, volunteer socialization

*This case study is based on research published in *Management Communication Quarterly* that was conducted in three organizational contexts (advocacy for abused children, ministry to at-risk youth, and fire safety and rescue services). This particular scenario involves only two contexts but was informed by observations and interviews with volunteers and supervisors in each context.

CHAPTER NINE

The Ethics OF Marketing THE Marginalized

A Case Study of Heifer International*

LINDSEY B. ANDERSON
University of Maryland

ROBIN PATRIC CLAIR
Purdue University

Luke was sitting in the reception area of Heifer International excited to start his first day on the job as its new public relations coordinator. He quickly checked his watch as his new manager, Stephanie, walked in the door. "Hi, Luke. How is our new public relations specialist?"

Luke stood up and shook Stephanie's hand. He had met Stephanie several times during the interview process and was really looking forward to working with her. "I'm great, Stephanie," Luke responded. "I'm ready to learn more about Heifer and my responsibilities."

Stephanie ushered Luke through a maze of cubicles into a small conference room. "We're going to work in here today, since I want to cover the culture of Heifer before you start working on our public relations and advertising materials. I think you will find we have quite an altruistic mission."

Luke took out a legal pad and pen and prepared to take notes. Stephanie took a deep breath and started. "Heifer began during the Spanish Civil War when an American farmer, Dan West, volunteered for the Church of the Brethren in Spain. As he rationed cups of milk to malnourished children as part of his volunteer work, he realized that the children didn't need a cup of milk; they needed a cow. This simple idea grew into a small nonprofit organization that is now Heifer International. It started small. In 1944, West supplied 17 heifers to the poor of Puerto Rico.[1] Today we have helped more than 20 million families around the world."[2]

"Our recipients have to make just one promise to receive a livestock gift—to pass it on by giving the animal's offspring to other families in need. 'Passing on the gift' is a key phrase here at Heifer, since it is our primary strategy to eradicate hunger and poverty and to replenish the earth. I know what you're thinking; ending poverty is a large feat, and I agree, but it's not an unrealistic goal. Just imagine all of the people we have helped already."

Luke looked up from his legal pad and nodded at Stephanie in agreement. He thought to himself that it was so inspiring to work at an organization like Heifer, a place where the main priority was to help the poor.

Stephanie took a sip of water and then continued. "We have a really strong public relations and advertising department. Heifer's promotional materials have received multiple awards. Just a few years ago, we received several prestigious Addy Awards for our marketing messages.[3] The advertising community seemed really impressed with our book, *One World, One Family*, the annual catalogues, and our web-based content. I'm excited for you to learn the ropes and start making contributions to our materials."

"Me, too," said Luke as he leaned back in his chair. "Me, too."

****

A few weeks later, Luke sat in his cubicle looking at a contact sheet that he was given by a staff photographer. He glanced up and made eye contact with his coworker Hannah. "Hey, Hannah, can you help me choose a photo for the holiday catalogue? I'm working on the *Boxes, Bows, and Buffalo* section."

"Sure," replied Hannah as she walked over to Luke's cubicle and began looking at the contact sheet. Hannah was a more experienced member of the public relations and advertising team, and Luke respected her opinion.

Luke started to talk through his concerns as Hannah continued to look through a magnifying glass. "I am just concerned that the people in these photos look too happy and the setting is very idyllic. It just doesn't reflect the way I imagine the poor looking."

"I understand," said Hannah, "but in our materials, the poor should never be portrayed in a state of abject poverty. We don't want them to be seen as beggars, but rather small-business entrepreneurs or small-farm farmers or ranchers who

1   Heifer International. (n.d.). History. Retrieved from http://www.heifer.org/ourwork/our-history

2   Heifer International. (n.d.). Ending hunger and poverty. Retrieved from http://www.heifer.org/ending-hunger/index.html

3   Heifer International. (n.d.). Awards and acknowledgments. Retrieved from http://www.heifer.org/ourwork/success/awards

just need a little bit of help to get their business or farm running. And most of the photos that I have seen are like the ones on this contact sheet, which are shot in lush green landscapes on a sunny day."

Luke smiled at Hannah and nodded. Hannah looked back down and offered more advice. "You also need to pay attention to the gift that we are providing in these materials. The focus should be on the animal itself or a by-product of the animal. For example, I'm working on the *Gift of Honeybees* section and I just chose a photograph of a young boy smiling between large bottles of honey. I think it shows that we are providing more than a swarm of bees to the boy's family, but also a means of income for the recipients. It really helps encourage people to donate money, because the gift keeps giving."

Hannah pushed away from the desk and pointed at a small square in the center of the contact sheet. "I think this is the photo you need for your section."

Luke thanked Hannah and grabbed the contact sheet to get a closer look at the selected photo. As it came into focus, Luke saw that the frame contained a picture of a woman with a pink pashmina draped over her shoulders. She was smiling at the camera as she fed the water buffalo a handful of grass. Behind her were several hay bales and a goat in front of a small shed with a thatched roof.

"Okay," said Luke. He then thought to himself, "Now I just need to write a narrative to accompany the photo, one that explains why she is so happy." He looked down at his notes on the woman in the pink pashmina and started to write her story. He knew that he wanted to remain consistent with the narratives that appeared in previous holiday catalogues, so he focused on the struggles that she overcame because of Heifer's gift. He started by sharing that her family was on the brink of starvation and then highlighted that after receiving a water buffalo, her family had not only enough milk to drink, but more than enough to sell, thus providing money for other necessities. The woman's family passed on the gift by giving the calf from their water buffalo to another needy family, which completed the gift-giving cycle. As Luke wrapped up his narrative, he thought, "There, that should explain why she is smiling."

The next day, Luke came into the office with two cups of coffee. "Good morning, Hannah." He handed her the steaming beverage and asked, "Do you have a couple of minutes to talk?"

Hannah smiled, saying, "I needed this pick-me-up. Of course we can chat. What's wrong?"

"Nothing's wrong," replied Luke. "I have just been thinking about the way our materials show our livestock recipients."

He looked at Hannah, who was blowing the steam off her coffee. "What do you mean?" she asked.

Luke paused before stating, "I just feel as though both the photographs and stories combine to give a particular impression of the poor. But that impression is partial and pasteurizes the life of the people being portrayed. You know, caring for a water buffalo and farming are tough jobs. It's as if we're hiding the 'dirty work.' Our recipients must spend so much time milking the water buffalo and shoveling manure for fertilizer, but this reality is not mentioned in the narrative we write or depicted in the photographs that we choose. In fact, the pictures and the stories both minimize the actual work that goes along with receiving one of our gifts."

"That's true," responded Hannah, "but I think donors want to see the positive outcomes of donating, not the actual work involved in raising cattle." Hannah took a swig of her coffee and then added, "You know, the type of work Heifer recipients engage in is just so different than most of our donors."

"Who are our donors?" inquired Luke.

Hannah tilted her head and said, "White-collar workers, for the most part. But I'm just thinking about the income differences between the two groups. Our donors don't just engage in different work, but they make so much more money than the recipients." Hannah paused briefly before leaving Luke with one final thought. "You know, our CEO salary was over $250,000 a couple of years ago. That is more money than our recipients will ever see, and he made that in one year."

****

A couple of months later, Luke received the final version of the catalogue in the mail. He had just arrived home from work after a long day, so he tossed the glossy book on the kitchen table and sat down on his couch to watch the evening news. He then heard his phone ring. He looked down and saw that it was his mother, Libby, calling. He picked up.

"Hi, Luke!" exclaimed his mother. "The Heifer holiday catalogue arrived, and it looks great. I am so proud of you."

"Thanks, Mom. I only handled a couple of sections though. A whole team of us created the catalogue," Luke explained.

"Well, it looks great. In fact, your father and I want to buy a pig for a family from Haiti. What do you think? I just want to help end poverty," said Libby.

"Mom, you know you can't solve the global issue of poverty by donating one pig, right? This is just a small step to possibly help a couple of people. I'm not even sure how effective it is when you think about how much it costs to raise a farm animal before it becomes profitable," Luke confided.

Luke heard Libby sigh as he went on. "Second, you won't actually get to pick out a recipient or a particular gift, like baby chicks, a lamb, or a pig. Look at the fine print in the catalogue. It explains that we do not actually give the gift to the individual you selected, but rather the donation is given to a unique community effort. In short, I believe the money goes to a bank, where it is bundled with other donations, and the banks then distribute the money by way of purchasing commodities, livestock, or paying for programs. The money may still be going to a good cause, but the idea that you can choose what and to whom your donation will go is an illusion to increase donations."

Libby paused for a moment. "Well, honey, do you think I should donate a pig to a family in rural Haiti or not?"

KEY TERMS

Art of Illusion - the art of illusion refers to the strategies and tactics invoked to misdirect someone's attention.

Dirty Work - jobs or specific work-related tasks that are seen as physically, morally, and/or socially disgusting or degrading. This type of work varies in terms of the perceived level of "dirtiness" (e.g., a sanitation worker and a nurse). Culture also influences which jobs are seen as "dirty."

Ethics - ethics relates to questions of morals. The original term is drawn from the Greek word for ethos, which refers to one's character, especially in terms of being honorable, honest, and credible.

Metonymy - metonymy refers to a literary trope used to name someone or something by relying on an attribute as a substitution. Relying on one attribute to define someone or something necessarily provides a partial portrayal.

Microfinance - microfinance is the practice of lending small amounts of money via specific lending institutions to individuals who may not otherwise be able to obtain a loan from a local bank because of financial challenges. It is most often practiced in "developing" countries.

DISCUSSION QUESTIONS

1. What are the ethical issues surrounding a nonprofit organization's partial portrayal of the poor? That is, if an NPO uses metonymy to produce marketing materials that do not necessarily represent the people, conditions, situations, and needs in a realistic manner, do the ends justify the means? Why or why not?

2. What are acceptable CEO salaries for NPOs? What are the criteria on which salaries should be based? Does the nature of NPO services and service recipients make a difference? Why or why not?

3. What ethical decisions surround an NPO's creation of marketing and fundraising messages? What responsibility do potential donors have to think critically or conduct their own research about social issues?

4. To what extent is the practice of suggesting that the donor is picking out a specific "gift" for a specific family, the art of illusion, misleading or unethical? To what extent should donors be able to know and direct how their dollars are used by an NPO?

5. How did Heifer use metonymy in its portrayal of the poor? How do we use metonymy on an everyday basis to describe people?

6. Many jobs are considered "dirty." Some jobs may be devalued as a result of being considered "dirty." Identify some "dirty" jobs that are and are not looked down upon. What reasons may explain the difference? How might Heifer International's marketing materials look different if they included the hard work of raising animals—work that some people might consider "dirty"?

SUGGESTED READINGS

Clair, R. P. (2013, June). Toward a theory of metonymy with implications for "the poor." Paper presented at the annual International Communication Association conference. London, UK.

Clair, R. P., & Anderson, L. B. (2013). Portrayals of the poor on the cusp of capitalism: Promotional materials in the case of Heifer International. *Management Communication Quarterly, 27,* 537–567. doi: 10.1177/0893318913502773

Dempsey, S. E. (2009). NGOs, communicative labor, and the work of grassroots representation. *Communication and Critical/Cultural Studies, 6,* 328–345. doi: 10.1080/14791420903348625

Drew, S. K., Mills, M., & Gassaway, B. (Eds.). (2007). *Dirty work: The social construction of taint.* Waco, TX: Baylor University Press.

Finnegan, C. A. (2003). *Picturing poverty: Print culture and FSA photographs.* Washington, DC: Smithsonian Institution Press.

Novak, D. R., & Harter, L. M. (2008). "Flipping the scripts" of poverty and panhandling: Organizing democracy by creating connections. *Journal of Applied Communication Research, 36,* 391–414. doi: http://dx.doi.org/10.1080/00909880802104890

KEYWORDS

ethics, metonymy, dirty work, art of illusion, microfinance

*This case study was developed using data from a research study conducted by Clair and Anderson (2013). In this article, the authors analyzed Heifer International's organizational website and holiday catalogues to uncover the ways that Heifer portrayed the recipients in its promotional materials to encourage "gift giving." Heifer used photographs, titles, narrative statements, and supporting discourse to create and sustain a "pasteurized" image of the poor that showed them as entrepreneurs who are happy, healthy, and living in idyllic locations. Heifer relied on three rhetorical strategies: (1) perspective by incongruity, (2) dissoi logoi/kairos, and (3) the art of illusion to maintain a perceived balance between charity work and capitalism.

CHAPTER TEN

"True Believer's" Blues

Betrayal, Hypocrisy, and Mission Drift in Nonprofit Work*

SHERIANNE SHULER

Creighton University

Aaron sank into his chair, sighing loudly as he rubbed his eyes. "I guess it didn't go well?" asked Jane, his office mate.

"Why am I surprised?" he asked. "Why do I continue to get my hopes up only to see all I hold dear assaulted? It was all I could do not to punch Keith in the mouth."

"Where did you leave it?" Jane asked gently.

"I told him we'd talk tomorrow and got out of there before I said something to get myself fired," Aaron replied.

Aaron and Jane had been good friends for four years, working at Rural School Progress Association (RSPA) first as graduate student assistants and later as professional staff. RSPA, a nonacademic unit of a research university, had evolved in 25 years, but there were some constants: passion for schools in rural communities, a belief that local people know best what they need, and a commitment to provide advocacy and resources to help rural schools avoid closure and consolidation.

The underlying philosophy that "local people know best" set RSPA apart from many university "outreach" programs. Despite good intentions, many such programs send the patronizing message that "we at the university have all the answers about what you need." RSPA's empowering mission was an article of faith for employees and rural constituents, and was particularly appealing to funders underwriting programs. RSPA worked with rural teachers, specifically, because they believed rural teachers and schools delivered excellent education when provided with proper support. If rural schools were able to avoid closure or consolidation, their surrounding communities retained a crucial sense of pride and connection.

Aaron loved working with other passionate progressives who found in their work a "life purpose" and a "chance to make real change." Although highly educated and living in a college town, he came from a working-class background and was fiercely committed to preserving the positives of rural life in his state. Initially, Aaron was captivated by RSPA's philosophy and by Keith, the founding director. He described Keith as "a really charismatic guy. He comes across as intelligent, with great ideas about good work we could do. It was a case of hero worship, for sure." As Aaron became more involved with students, teachers, and community members, he became what his coworker Rob called "a true believer." He and other true believers who worked at RSPA shared a collective passion about their work. They loved and lived it.

Aaron now kicked himself as questions swirled in his head. How had he tolerated Keith's betrayals for so long? Why hadn't he followed his former coworker, Deborah, and left earlier? She warned him about how Keith had changed, and Aaron witnessed how shabbily Deborah was treated. For a while, he justified sticking around to continue the work he felt called to do. "No longer," he thought.

Aaron once thought he'd be at RSPA forever. Last year, Keith confided his desire to groom Aaron and Jane as the next director and assistant director. Though surprised at the vote of confidence given their short tenure at RSPA, Aaron and Jane enjoyed dreaming about what good work they could do together.

Aaron, like most RSPA employees, lived on "soft money." This meant his meager salary was funded by grants, while the university only provided benefits. Aaron had been excited to write a National Science Foundation (NSF) grant to hopefully bring in substantial money for programs and also a more comfortable salary for him. Maybe he could finally save for a house down payment or replace his old truck, expenses not possible with his current income. In consultation with rural teachers, Aaron submitted a preliminary grant proposal that was favorably received with an invitation to submit a full proposal. With enthusiasm, he gathered an advisory board of teachers, as per RSPA policy.

At the meeting, however, every single teacher said, "We don't have time. This isn't something that would really benefit us much. We don't want to move forward." He tried convincing them, but the teachers didn't believe the grant was what their schools needed. Although this dealt a disappointing blow, Aaron was committed to RSPA's philosophy that rural teachers and community members know best. When he returned to the office that afternoon, he told Keith, "This ends it. If you've got the teachers telling you this ain't a good idea … we don't do it." The news was not well received.

Later that night, Aaron sat on Rob's porch, drinking and venting to his former roommate. Rob, who worked in another area of RSPA, was married to Jane. The three had started together, and Aaron was relieved their close relationships hadn't diminished when his two best friends married.

"Well, I know one thing. God gave us Maker's Mark and cheap cigars for situations like this," Rob offered.

I'll drink to that," Aaron agreed as they raised their glasses.

After draining his bourbon and pouring another, Aaron recounted his conversation with Keith. "I told him what happened and he's like, 'Well, I don't care what they said—we're going to write this grant. They don't understand or have the vision of what this could be. We're going ahead with this.' He wasn't even attempting to hold to the rhetoric of 'teachers know best.' He basically said, 'Screw those folks; we've got to get some money.'"

"His hypocrisy is not surprising," Rob said. "That's similar to what happened to Deborah awhile back."

"EXACTLY!" Aaron exclaimed. "It's the same thing! Use the philosophy to sound impressive for grant proposals, but ignore it when it actually counts. The man has totally abandoned everything he used to stand for."

"Yep," Rob replied and then continued. "Remember when they got that little planning grant? It was exciting because it would fund preparations for a multimillion-dollar grant proposal. Deborah assumed they would include rural schools in their planning, but Keith wanted her to just do the proposal. Deborah was pretty insistent, saying, 'No, we have to go to the schools and ask.' And Keith said, 'We don't have time,' and I won't ever forget this, he said, 'They won't know what to do anyway.' That was completely out of character—he'd never been like that before."

Aaron shook his head, saying, "I guess I've been hoping he'd snap out of it and go back to the 'Good Keith' who hired me. I feel so disillusioned, like everything I've worked for and believed in here was a big huge lie."

There was a long silence as Rob blew some rings of cigar smoke before reflecting, "You know, I haven't had a major conflict like this come up. I guess my 'true believerism' has been challenged little by little, when I would think, 'Well, that doesn't quite go along with the philosophy,' but anytime I brought it up, it would calm my fears to hear Keith or one of his lackeys say, 'Sometimes you have to push a little.' Cuz I thought, 'Well, okay, that makes sense.' Everybody gets complacent; that doesn't mean that you think somebody's stupid, or anything else. Maybe somebody's just scared to do something. And so, just give 'em a little push, like, 'Come on, you can do this.' But that grew thin, pretty quickly, when I realized, 'Wait a minute. You're basically telling me all we're doing is pushing around here. We shouldn't have to push that much.'"

Aaron sat upright and pointed his cigar at Rob, exclaiming, "Yes! I hold Keith more responsible, but he's not alone. I remember talking to his buddy Scott about rural teachers, and you know, RSPA has always publically honored teachers in rural schools. To me, it always seemed a bit self-sacrificial that they would choose that life. But Scott said that lots of teachers went into teaching in rural places because they couldn't do anything else. If they were smarter, they would either do something else or they would go somewhere else. I remember I kind of got a chill running up my spine."

"I thought I might find you two out here! Why do you have a chill running up your spine?" Jane asked as she joined them on the porch. She had been working late, and now plopped down on the porch swing inquiring, "Have I missed anything earth-shattering?"

"Only Aaron's spirit is shattered, hopefully not the whole earth," Rob quipped. Jane rolled her eyes. Rob continued. "I've often wondered if because this is our first job, we're all going to be stunted for life in some way."

Aaron sighed. "I swear, I want my next job to be something I don't care about. In a factory or something."

Rob laughed. "Yeah, that's a nice fantasy, but both our dads did manual labor their whole lives, and that's why they pushed us to go to college. It's easy to glamorize that work as more pure somehow, but there's problems there, too."

"Yeah, but at least I wouldn't have my passion and beliefs crapped on," Aaron countered.

"So, what are you going to do, Aaron?" Rob asked. "Is it time to go to the provost about the sham this place has become?"

Jane chimed in. "Of course that's tempting, the idea that everyone would find out RSPA is run by hypocrites who aren't following their own mission, but there's good work being done in the communities despite Keith and his soulless lackeys. The schools need us."

Aaron agreed, saying, "I know, which is why I'm feeling so pulled. I'd like to call up all the teachers or write a letter I cc to the provost that explains Keith's betrayals. Maybe even send it to funding agencies … but then a lot more people would get hurt. Not just kids and teachers who depend on us, but also our coworkers who really need their jobs. But if I just quit, probably nothing changes. Keith just writes that grant and the teachers think I've sold them out."

Jane nodded. "The thing is, this place WILL be exposed at some point. Someone at the university is going to start asking questions about how money is being spent. And Keith and his lackeys have gotten so wrapped up in raising money that they've stepped on toes in the communities. People there know they aren't getting much done."

Rob laughed. "I admit to a certain sense of wicked glee whenever something gets messed up these days. But it also makes me mad that they're ruining future chances to do good work in rural areas because people won't be so trusting next time."

Aaron agreed. "That's the part that makes me so sad. I love this work, but I think I'm not going to be able to keep doing it. Maybe we should start our own rural collective."

Jane nodded. "We could get Deborah back on board to raise tons of money and hire only the good people."

"Seriously, though, folks," Aaron interjected. "As much as I want to fantasize about that, I have a dilemma here. I need this job—I don't even have my résumé updated. But I can't continue this charade. I don't want to write that grant, and I don't want to tell the teachers their opinions don't matter."

"You could always hang around and pretend to write the grant while you look for another job—it certainly wouldn't be the first time people did nothing and collected checks around here," Rob joked.

Aaron replied, "Remind me when I'm looking for another job that I never want to feel this committed to my work again. I'm done being a true believer."

Jane laughed. "Yeah right, Aaron. You'd last two weeks in a job that didn't involve social justice. It's in your blood."

"I wonder if it's even possible to avoid being a true believer in my next job," Rob asked.

"I'm still a true believer," asserted Jane. "I think the philosophy is valid and it could work somewhere. Just not at RSPA."

Aaron stood up. "On that note, I need to head home. I hate to leave good company, but tomorrow is gonna come early." He said good night and walked to his truck, grateful for good friends who deeply understood his dilemma. "People without a sense of mission about their work don't have to deal with this," he thought as he hoisted himself into the truck. He noticed with a start that the clock on his dashboard read 11:47—he'd have to face Keith in just eight hours and was looking at a night with little sleep. As he backed down the driveway, he blasted Johnny Cash in the hopes that singing along to the "Folsom Prison Blues" might make him forget his own.

KEY TERMS

Mission Drift - the tendency for organizations to gradually and usually inadvertently alter their activities away from their original values and goals.

Organizational Dissent - the multiple ways an employee recognizes and decides whether and how to voice disagreement with organizational practices or policies.

Organizational Socialization - the process by which an individual "learns the ropes" of how things are done in a particular organization or, more broadly, learns societal expectations relating to work.

DISCUSSION QUESTIONS

1. What are the pros and cons of Aaron's options for dealing with this situation?
2. If Aaron and/or his coworkers voice(s) their dissent, how could he/they do it productively?
3. Is Keith justified in pushing Aaron to write the grant, or will this mission drift be detrimental to RSPA? Is it appropriate for NPOs to stray from their stated mission to obtain funding? Why or why not?
4. RSPA's philosophy is "local people know best." Do you agree with this philosophy? Under what circumstances should an NPO impose its ideas on the people it serves?
5. The characters talk a lot about "true believerism." How important is it that nonprofit employees and volunteers are passionate about the organization's mission? Have you ever been a "true believer" and then felt betrayed by the hypocrisy of a leader/organization? How did you deal with it?
6. The characters wondered how their first jobs would impact their future organizational experiences. Think about your earliest organizational socialization (as an employee or volunteer). How might those experiences (good and bad) impact your future career?

SUGGESTED READINGS

Dees, J. G., & Anderson, B. B. (2003). Sector-bending: Blurring lines between nonprofit and for-profit. *Society, 40*, 16–27. doi: 10.1007/s12115-003-1014-z.

Garner, J. T. (2013). Dissenters, managers, and coworkers: The process of co-constructing organizational dissent and dissent effectiveness. *Management Communication Quarterly, 27*, 373–395. doi: 10.1177/0893318913488946

Scott, C., & Myers, K. (2010). Toward an integrative theoretical perspective on organizational membership negotiations: Socialization, assimilation, and the duality of structure. *Communication Theory, 20*, 79–105. doi: 10.1111/j.1468-2885.2009.01355.x

KEYWORDS

betrayal, hypocrisy, mission drift, organizational dissent, organizational socialization

*This case study was constructed from an extended focus group interview conducted with four former RSPA employees that generated a 69-page single-spaced transcript. When possible, the participants' actual language is used in the case's reconstructed dialogue. The names of people and organizations are changed to protect their identities.

Boards OF Directors: Managing Roles, Decisions, AND Stakeholders

CHAPTER ELEVEN

Joining A New Nonprofit Board OF Directors

Beginning with the Strategic Plan*

TRUDY MILBURN
Independent Researcher

ALAN HANSEN
Carroll College

As Theresa drove into the parking lot, she thought back to what happened two months prior, when she attended a meeting of the Parent Teacher Association (PTA) at her daughter's charter school and heard about the formation of a new nonprofit foundation. Theresa had been interested in nonprofit organizations before, so her interest was piqued, and she listened closely.

The woman speaking identified herself as Bev, a former schoolteacher and the organization's first paid staff member. Bev was recruiting volunteers to help organize this new nonprofit foundation. She explained that the charter school was initially created to occupy space on the local college campus. While land had been set aside on the campus, they now needed to mobilize support to make the charter school happen. The foundation was being formed to ensure that the charter school moved to the college campus.

Thinking back to the night she met Bev, Theresa realized that she didn't take long to consider Bev's proposal. The charter school currently occupied a vacated building that the school district recently closed because of low enrollment—a temporary arrangement that could change at any time if they chose to place another school in the building. Theresa recalled the charter school principal explaining that the charter school operated outside the jurisdiction of typical public schools and leased the building year to year. At the time, Theresa's impression was that the facility was getting old and the charter school would need to invest quite a bit for upkeep if it stayed. Theresa remembered weighing the driving distance to take her daughter to school from the college campus, calculating that it would be much closer than driving to the current run-down and temporary building. In the end, it seemed an easy decision to add her name to the sign-up sheet seeking new board members.

It was two months ago that Theresa was invited to attend the first meeting, based simply on her signing up during the PTA meeting. At that meeting, 15 people, including charter school teachers and the principal, parents, and even professors from the local college, enthusiastically communicated their passion for the charter school and were immediately added as board members. Since that time, Theresa learned that the charter school was a "professional development" school, according to an education faculty member on the board, in which college students studying to become teachers spend time in the classroom with the children and use the most up-to-date principles and methods for teaching and learning. Theresa recalled leaving the first meeting excited to be part of this new endeavor. As she entered the building for tonight's meeting, Theresa realized that joining this new nonprofit organization as a board member was as simple as showing up.

Strategic Planning Meeting

It was 6:50 p.m. on a Thursday evening. Walking into the school's library, Theresa observed bookshelves lining the walls and large tables with chairs where the others were assembling. This second meeting of the charter school's board seemed similar to the first. Theresa grabbed a copy of each handout and her name tent while heading to her seat. She greeted Bev, who she learned was always the first to arrive. Other board members arrived, and the meeting began with a request from Bev that everyone grab a copy of the agenda, bylaws, and handouts.

Bev introduced the facilitator, Bob, a professor from the local college's business school who was brought in to help the board craft a strategic plan—a requirement for all new organizations. When the facilitator asked the first question, Joan (a retired principal), Peter (a real estate developer and president of the Board of Directors), and Bev—all founding members of the board—were the first to respond with answers and opinions.

Having served on other boards, Theresa was accustomed to rehashing the mission of the organization during the first part of any strategic planning meeting. Even though the mission was always written down, she had heard facilitators explain useful reasons for discussing it as a group. Bob set the context by defining key terms from one of the handouts:

"The mission is the reason why we exist and the vision is where we want to be. The general strategy constitutes activities the organization engages in that support the mission. In order to figure out which activities to engage in, organizations complete what we call a SWOT analysis."

Theresa glanced down at her handout and noticed the key terms: strengths, weaknesses, opportunities, and threats, creating the acronym SWOT. Bob continued:

"Whenever I ask a new group, 'Give me your top priorities,' people often reply, 'Well, here are 25 things,' and I say, 'Well, you don't really have any priorities.' Of course, out of these 25 things, people can only do one or two things. But the key to any organization is to focus on one or two things. If you don't focus, what happens is you must deal with these 10 or 12 things and then you end up in a mush. So you can't manage it, and you can't measure it. Of course, once organizational members determine their strategic activities, outside observers may still find fault with their plans. For instance, some plans are too detailed or contain too many steps. Some plans do not address who will be responsible for carrying out and accomplishing each activity indicated, and thus fail to specify the repercussions for not achieving the goals set forth."

As she listened to Bob, Theresa understood that the task of this meeting involved completing the worksheet by identifying each elements of the SWOT analysis as it applied to the organization. She asked herself, "Why has no one asked us to prepare for today's meeting with data or analysis?"

As the meeting progressed, Theresa observed that other board members did not seem troubled by this. They answered the questions with ease, in quick succession. Theresa wondered, "Being a new organization, how do we really know what the strengths, weaknesses, opportunities, and threats are yet? Why hasn't anyone thought to ask us to research these in comparable organizations in advance?" Theresa decided to dismiss these distracting thoughts and instead refocus on the conversation as it progressed. Just as she focused on the conversation, Peter, the president of the Board of Directors and a founding member of the organization, said:

"Raising money is not a mission. It may be a goal, but it's also an end. This analysis is meant to describe the end. What I want to focus on is, 'What are we going to spend the money on?' And I think if we're going to be successful in building a school on campus, that is going to have to be our priority focus. But there are other things that we can spend money on. For every dollar that comes in, though, we need to be very clear about where it's going. When I was at the Western State College, funds were designated to either a particular project or to be used for general purposes. So while this mission statement does not prohibit us from spending money on any one aspect of the project, we will need to get to the details through our strategic initiatives."

A bit later in the conversation, Peter interrupted an attempt by Bob to seek clarification in order to say the following: "But this statement describes exactly what we're all about. We should focus on fundraising not as an end, but as a means to get to an end."

At this point Joan, another founding board member, interjected:

"From the very beginning, we worked as fundraisers with the focus being on raising money for the project. Then we realized that we were more credible as a foundation, but we were really a committee that became a foundation. I just see so many positive things moving forward but with the stumbling block, which is way off in the future: that populations are going to take over these schools again. And then we won't have a home. Well, the facility we're sitting in is an example, right? It could be purchased or any number of things could happen. So am I right in saying that our goal is to raise money and support the school building? We are here to raise money. We have about three other boards that support the school in other ways. So we have a lot of other support. I think we are fundamentally here to raise money."

Peter rejoined:

"So we raise money and then somebody else makes the decision about how the funds are spent. Let's put it on the table: this is a foundation to raise money."

Bev then joined the conversational flow:

"This foundation transformed from the original vision of the facilities. It was to start fundraising, advocacy, and a movement towards building a school on the campus. The property is there. That's why this committee began a couple years ago. And that was the focus. Fundraising was a part of it, and advocacy was a part of it, along with policy and political action. So when you get into the foundation, its purpose is to raise money. I think what we're really struggling with right now: If we are raising money for that vision, then how does the money we raise go towards that vision? Or does the money we raise go directly to the operation of the school?"

Theresa didn't take part in this line of discussion, leaving it mostly to other board members. Later in the conversation, she observed Cindy, a board member who had not participated in the interaction previously, who said:

"The end goal is the brand new $25 million building on the university campus. We're saying okay. That's the end goal. But in order to get to that end goal, we need to have a compelling program. So maybe the idea is, we need to fund our program first."

As she tried to digest what had been said so far, Theresa realized that anyone who continued to attend board meetings would be tacitly agreeing to raise money to finance a building. She considered carefully this proposition. Did she agree with the mission? Did she agree that this was what a charter school foundation should be doing? She couldn't help but feel that it made sense. From what she knew about foundations, they typically provided grants to those who applied. In this case, the foundation hadn't begun with a substantial endowment. Therefore, this must be the work of the organization. What the board needed to collectively determine was how the foundation could reach its goal, which, as Cindy had just reminded everyone, was $25 million.

Moreover, Theresa's impression of the founding board members and other new members was that while they seemed to have the best of intentions, no one aside from the three founding members (Peter, Bev, and Joan) seemed passionate or knowledgeable about fundraising. Theresa realized that meeting the substantial fundraising goal certainly would not happen with the kind of small fundraising events in which elementary schools commonly engaged: selling baked goods, tickets to performances, and so forth. In all, raising $25 million seemed like a wholly unrealistic goal from where Theresa was sitting.

Later in the meeting, Bev interpreted the prior conversation as indicative of the need to form three subcommittees to accomplish the foundation's work. She labeled these subcommittees Marketing and Public Relations (PR), Legislation and Advocacy, and Fundraising and Development. If divided evenly, these subcommittees would include five members each. At the conclusion of the planning meeting, three board members were each designated, or volunteered, to direct a particular subcommittee to meet before the next board meeting. Bev asked if Theresa would be willing to lead the Marketing and PR subcommittee and coordinate their first meeting.

Accordingly, before the meeting ended, Theresa had to decide on several things. The primary question was whether or not she believed enough in the mission of this new nonprofit organization to continue as a board member. The second question related to her willingness and ability to competently lead the Marketing and PR subcommittee. As the conversation from the planning meeting was focused primarily on the mission, neither the structure of the organization nor the specific fundraising activities had been worked out yet, so planning Marketing and PR seemed a bit premature. To Theresa, this new organization began to seem like too much work with too little to gain. However, she had come this far and felt as if the organization was gaining momentum. What should be done?

KEY TERMS

Board Member - an elected member of the Board of Directors of an organization or agency.

Organizational Mission - the guiding statement toward which organizations strive.

Strategic Planning - a process by which executives or board members work out how the goals of an organization will be achieved within a specified period of time.

SWOT Analysis - one technique used within strategic planning to help organizational members define the strengths and weaknesses of their value proposition in comparison to their competitors.

DISCUSSION QUESTIONS

1. Often people begin participating in an organization that has a well-established mission. How is this new nonprofit organization defining its mission? Do you think it can be accomplished? Why or why not?
2. At some point in the meeting, Theresa realizes that there are things about this organization, and board, that she needs to understand even before she can properly decide whether or not to continue with the board. What are some of the aspects she should consider?
3. Considering the dialogue above, how might the following aspects of the meeting be important in helping Theresa decide if she should continue as a board member: who speaks first; who speaks most often; and who seems most assertive in directing the interaction?
4. What values do the participants appear to hold, as demonstrated by their contributions to the meeting? Discuss those held by Bev, Peter, and Theresa in particular. How might differing values influence decisions, interactions, and outcomes?
5. What is the role of a facilitator during meetings? What rhetorical strategies could the facilitator, Bob, use to help board members work together more effectively?
6. Organizational documents or other objects invoked by participants in conversations might actually play a part in the trajectory of interaction. How would you describe the role that organizational objects (i.e., mission statement, bylaws, etc.) play in this interaction?
7. To what extent are the members collaborating to accomplish shared goals? Using a theory of organizing or interaction, justify your response.

SUGGESTED READINGS

Boden, D. (1994). *The business of talk: Organizations in action.* Cambridge, MA: Polity Press.

Milburn, T. (2009). *Nonprofit Organizations: Creating Membership through Communication.* Cresskill, NJ: Hampton Press.

Sprain, L., & Boromisza-Habashi, D. (2012). Meetings: A cultural perspective. *Journal of Multicultural Discourses, 7*(2), 179–189. doi: 10.1080/17447143.2012.685743

Yancey, P. (2000). *Parents founding charter schools: Dilemmas of empowerment and decentralization.* New York, NY: Peter Lang.

KEYWORDS

board member, strategic planning, organizational mission

*The first author has been a participant-observer within four Boards of Directors. The first two formed the corpus of the book *Nonprofit Organizations: Creating Membership through Communication*, published by Hampton Press in 2009. The conversational segments for the present case were derived from participant-observation research conducted in 2007–2009 as a board member for a new 501(c)(3) foundation for a charter school on the West Coast. Elected as recording secretary, the first author obtained permission to audio record each meeting, take minutes, and use the data for research purposes.

CHAPTER TWELVE

Hope FOR THE Future*

STACY TYE-WILLIAMS AND JOANNE M. MARSHALL

Iowa State University

Jan often thinks about the professional development meeting she attended in 2005 when she and a group of fellow teachers learned about the extent of poverty and homelessness in their school district. They were all shocked to learn that in their community of 26,000 people, 21 students were homeless. Students in the community were reaching out to teachers and cafeteria workers for basic necessities like winter coats and extra food to take home for the weekend so they didn't go hungry. "This is unacceptable. We have to do something about it," Jan, a longtime high school English teacher, shared with her coworkers.

Her friend Nancy was sympathetic. "I agree with you, but we're already strapped for time as it is. I know you are the champion of good causes, but honestly what can *we* do?" Jan spent a sleepless night pondering just that question.

Creation of the Hope Foundation

The next day in the break room, Jan approached a few coworkers with her idea. "I couldn't sleep last night because all I could think about were our homeless students," Jan said. "I just don't understand how we didn't know how much some of the families in our district are struggling. But I came up with a plan. We will organize a silent auction of donated gift baskets. For example, someone could donate a 'Tea Time' basket complete with various varieties of tea, mugs, and a kettle. All of the proceeds will go to help families in our community. When teachers recognize a student need, they will come to one of us to nominate them for help. Families cannot ask us directly for help; they have to be nominated by a member of the school staff. We will be the board. Ultimately, we will provide onetime help to families in need. I would like to have our event right around Christmas so people can purchase the baskets for holiday gifts. That leaves us a little over a month to make it happen. So, who is with me?"

Nancy and Claire both agreed to help. "It will be difficult, but it might also be really fun," Nancy said.

Growing Hope

Jan and the teachers of Glenview Community School formed what they eventually called the Hope Foundation. The first year they had a goal of raising $1,000 to help students and their families. Instead, they were able to raise almost $15,000, and they helped about 30 families. Now, almost 10 years later, with the help of other teachers and community members, they have given away roughly $280,000, and they help over 100 families each year. The mission of the Hope Foundation is to help struggling families get by and to show them that their educators care about them. To that end, families have received help in the form of gas cards to help absorb the cost of traveling to medical treatments, onetime rent and mortgage payments, utility payments, and groceries, to name just a few.

Over the years, the foundation overcame many challenges. At first, people in the community didn't know anything about them or the resources they provided. They had to communicate their mission to the school community, the town, and families who might need assistance. Building community trust was an important part of their growth and success. Part of that trust came from having an established core group involved in organizing the foundation into a 501(c)(3) organization. Community members knew that the money they donated was being used to help people in their community instead of going to administrative overhead or being sent to help people outside the community.

Another challenge the foundation overcame was creating a system that could move quickly so help didn't get tied down in bureaucratic red tape. They recognized that if a child needed a winter coat, she didn't need it in a few months; she needed it immediately. Once a school staff member referred a family to the foundation board, they generally were able to approve the request and fill the need within 24–48 hours. This quick turnaround was accomplished through meticulous record keeping, frequent face-to-face and e-mail communication between members, and a shared understanding of rules for who they help and how. The foundation asked teachers and staff to keep their eyes and ears open to student and community needs. For example, if a student didn't complete homework because her electricity was shut off and she didn't have light to read her book, the teacher told a board member, and the board checked records and communicated about whether or not to approve the request. Once approved for assistance, a member of the board contacted the utility company for the balance and provided a check directly to the utility company. All members were informed about support provided. If there were any questions about resources or support, members consulted with one another to reach mutual agreement.

Although they had experienced quite a bit of turnover for peripheral roles like web designer, most of the original foundation board had remained intact, even though two of the members, Jan and Nancy, were now retired. Despite these changes and challenges, they worked well together over the years, and the organization ran smoothly. They believed they worked so well together because of their different strengths. Jan always joked that she likes the party, but Nancy and Claire pay attention to the technical elements of the foundation. Jan readily told others that she may be the idea person, but without detail-oriented members like Nancy and Claire, they would fail. The board was proud of their accomplishments but also realized that some changes needed to be made to strengthen the organization even more, especially as their leadership retires from teaching. They decided to discuss the challenges they were facing in a special meeting.

The Meeting

Jan called their meeting to order and shared their year-end summary. "As you know, last year was one of our best ones yet. We raised almost $40,000. We had many referrals from teachers and helped 102 families. Overall, I think we had a fantastic year." Jan paused while they gave each other high fives, and then continued. "We have come so far since our first year of not really knowing what we were doing. Can you imagine trying to get the event off the ground in one month now? Crazy!" Jan exclaimed. "That being said, it's time to start talking about this year's Hope Festival," she continued. "Claire, how are basket sign-ups going?"

"Good overall," explained Claire. "However, it seems like our donations are down a bit. There have also been fewer people signing up to help on our Google Doc."

Claire hesitated, so Nancy picked up where she trailed off. "Well, I think we need to reorient the teachers about what we do and what we need. We need to work on getting them more involved. They are usually happy to help out, but just like everyone, they are busy, so we need to give them a nudge to help each year. I think now that two of us are retired, it does impact our connection to the school just by us not physically being there. I really do."

"I have thought a lot about that." Jan sighed. "We are a complex little 'business.' If we do transition out of active roles in the foundation, we have to have people on the board who can maintain our standards of confidentiality. We don't want someone who will blab about the families we have helped. We also need people who will stay on for a while. The leadership on the board can't change every year, or there won't be consistency. Our foundation works because the teachers know who to contact if they have a family who needs our help, and they trust us. If people change every year, teachers won't know who to go to, and the organization will suffer. At the same time, I understand that we can't do this forever. We have been doing this for almost 10 years now. Maybe it's time for us to move on. I'm really torn. I love what we have created together and really don't want to see it go up in a puff of smoke, especially when I know how much the Hope Foundation has benefited our community. Plus, I would miss working with all of you! It's just hard because this is our baby. I realize that my vision might not be the same vision as a new person's vision, but their heart might still be in it just as much. It's just hard to think about someone else raising our baby. Claire, what do you think?"

After a brief pause, Claire stated, "I have also sensed a bit of a change since you both retired. Jan, you are so good at getting people involved and motivated to help, so some of that momentum seems to be missing. What we need is another *you* in the school!" Everyone laughed at the idea of another Jan. She really was fearless when it came to asking people for donations or to help with their annual event. Claire continued. "All kidding aside, I cannot imagine the Hope Foundation without all of us together. Plus, I know the community really respects the way we do things, and I would worry that changes might result in a loss of community support. Without that, we would really be in trouble." They all nodded their heads in agreement. Over the years the community had shown an outpouring of support. Even though it wasn't a wealthy community, people were more than willing to donate money, gift baskets, supplies, publicity, and other resources.

"No matter what we decide," Nancy continued, "we have to figure out how to get the teachers more involved this year so we can have another successful event. We spend so much time and effort recruiting volunteers each year. It would be nice if people would just help out each year."

"I really think a lot of it comes down to teachers being busy already. Let's face it; we all know firsthand that teachers are constantly being asked to help out in the community on their own time," Jan shared. "Wow! We have identified some major issues to think about. We are facing a bit of a crossroads. We have been very successful over the past 10 years, but we need to think about the next 10 years. The membership of the board is something we need to explore together to determine what makes the most sense for the organization moving forward. Getting and keeping volunteers is also an issue we need to address. In the interest of time, let's table our discussion of both of these issues for today. Please do some thinking on these items and let's discuss them again at our meeting next month." They all agreed to discuss it at the next meeting and moved on to discuss their annual event.

Changing of the Guard

Jan left the meeting excited about their upcoming event but also with a bit of a heavy heart. "I know one day I will have to step down from my role in the foundation," she thought. "But who will replace me? It has to be a certain type of person." She let out an audible sigh. "Maybe we should ask if anyone is interested in being the leader of the board. Or it might be better to recruit people we think would do a good job. Maybe we could form an advisory board of founding members to oversee the new group. I just hope we find people who want what is best for Hope. It would be a shame for the community to lose such a great resource because we didn't handle the transition well."

Ideas and possibilities began to swim around in her head. She was in for another sleepless night pondering how they could sustain the organization they created long into the future.

KEY TERMS

Bona Fide Group Perspective - group members belong to multiple groups simultaneously and these memberships influence and shape each other.

Grassroots Leadership - individuals who orchestrate action and change but who don't hold formal roles of power and authority.

Grassroots Organization - collection of people who come together at the local level to enact change and/or positively impact their community.

Transformational Leader - courageous change agents who inspire their followers to achieve organizational goals.

DISCUSSION QUESTIONS

Grassroots Organizations

1. What kinds of communication strategies are most appropriate for a grassroots organization like the Hope Foundation?
2. What are the strengths and/or weaknesses of the Hope Foundation as a grassroots organization?

Leadership

3. Is Jan an example of a transformational leader, or does she better resemble a founder with a vision? Why or why not?

4. Does the Hope Foundation need a transformational leader to take it new places once Jan steps down from her leadership role? Why or why not?

Group Membership

5. To what extent does the bona fide group perspective help to inform this case?
6. How should the Hope Foundation handle a possible shift in their board membership?
7. How should the Hope Foundation address their difficulty with recruiting and keeping volunteers?

Sustainability

8. The Hope Foundation has operated for 10 years. What recommendations do you have to help them continue to live out their mission for many more years to come?

SUGGESTED READINGS

Bass, B. M. (1990). From transactional to transformational leadership: Learning to share the vision. *Organizational Dynamics, 18*, 19–31. doi: 10.1016/0090-2616(90)90061-S

Jablin, F. M. (2001). Organizational entry, assimilation, and disengagement/exit. In F. M. Jablin & L. L. Putnam (Eds.), *The new handbook of organizational communication: Advances in theory, research, and methods* (pp. 732–818). Thousand Oaks, CA: Sage.

Kramer, M. W. (2011). Toward a communication model for the socialization of voluntary members. *Communication Monographs, 78*, 233–255. doi: 10.1080/03637751.2011.564640

Putnam, L. L., & Stohl, C. (1996). Bona fide groups: An alternative perspecitve for communication and decision making. In R. Y. Hirokawa & M. S. Poole (Eds.), *Communication and group decision making* (2nd ed.) (pp. 147–178). Thousand Oaks, CA: Sage.

Schutz, A., & Sandy, M. G. (2011). *Collective action for social change: An introduction to community organizing*. New York, NY: Palgrave Macmillan.

Willie, C. V., Ridini, S. P., & Willard, D. A. (Eds.). (2008). *Grassroots social action: Lessons in people power movements*. Lanham, MD: Rowman & Littlefield.

KEYWORDS

transformational leadership, grassroots leadership, grassroots organizations, bona fide group perspective, recruiting

*This case study is based on longitudinal research conducted on an organization created by a group of teachers in a small community to help families in their district. Interviews have taken place over the past three years. The data that inform this case come from a recent series of interviews with the founders of this organization. See also Marshall, J. M. (2012). Grassroots philanthrophy on the prairie. *Phi Delta Kappan, 93*(8), 34–38.

CHAPTER THIRTEEN

Meeting Madness*

JESSICA KATZ JAMESON
North Carolina State University

Donna shook her head as she drove home from the evening's board meeting. "I can't believe we spent 40 minutes on one item that should have been settled in two," she muttered to herself. Donna was the board president for Lily Day, a human services nonprofit organization that provided support for people who served as primary caregivers for adult family members with chronic illness. Their Board of Directors consisted of 12 members. Eight of the members were caregivers themselves, two were previous caregivers, and two were representatives from healthcare agencies. One board member was an attorney, one was an accountant, and one volunteered his time to coordinate the support programs and also served as a support group leader. There were two recently recruited board members of color (a Latina woman and an African American male).

While it is important for nonprofit boards to have members with a variety of backgrounds and expertise, it created some built-in conflict for the Lily Day board because of the different perspectives members brought to each meeting. Donna was especially concerned about the relationship between Martin, a caregiver, and Jeff, a former caregiver who also volunteered as a support group leader and the program coordinator. Both Jeff and Martin had served on the board for several years and often saw things differently. Because of their commitment to the organization and their tenure, they also had a tendency to dominate conversations. Each month the Board of Directors held a 90-minute meeting to govern the organization. Their responsibilities included setting policy, monitoring the organization's finances and programs, and ensuring the nonprofit was achieving its mission of helping family caregivers receive the social and psychological support needed to reduce stress and burnout and maintain the highest quality of life possible.

Board meetings were frequently stressful for Donna because she had a full-time job, two children, and cared for her mother, who suffered from early stage Alzheimer's. The last meeting became particularly heated, and the conversation was so confusing that the board secretary could not even keep track of whether a motion had been made, amended, or voted on. Donna was grateful that a researcher from a nearby university was recording their meetings and observing them for a study of board communication so she could try to reconstruct what happened later. For now, Donna felt frustrated that after all that discussion, they had ended up tabling the issue, and they would have to come back to it at next month's meeting. She could not help but wonder if there was anything she could have done differently to help the group come to an agreement rather than end in a stalemate. Her concerns were larger than this specific issue; she was also concerned about the potential for ongoing conflict between board members and their ability to work well together in the future.

A few days later, Donna contacted the researcher and asked if she could have a copy of the meeting transcript so she could help the board secretary reconstruct the minutes. She went straight to the part of the agenda where she had introduced the topic that triggered the difficult discussion:

Donna (President): We need to talk about a policy on publicizing support groups that are not directly Lily Day affiliated. I receive a lot of requests to promote other support activities, and I'm not sure how to respond to them.

Jeff (Senior Support Group Leader): I don't think we should be advertising any activities offered by people who have not been through our training. We have no idea what they are offering or any quality control.

Tony (Board Treasurer): Another problem is that sometimes a new program is offered, and then they stop and don't tell us.

Amanda (Provider): But what about support groups that have been around forever, and we know they are really popular? Shouldn't we let caregivers know about those?

Donna: Well, this is why we need to have a policy about how we're going to publicize groups like this. My initial thought was that we could have a listing on the website. We could also have a listing in the newsletter that is clearly delineated that says, "Here are some other resources that you might be interested in." Something to the effect of, "These are not specifically Lily Day resources. We're not …"

Eric (Family Member of Client and Attorney): Endorsing.

Donna: Yes, that's a good word. "We're not endorsing them, but we want to make this information available to you so that you can participate if you choose. We don't take any responsibility for the quality and the way the groups are run." This may be a good way to handle it. So what do you all think?

Glenn (Support Group Leader): I was just going to say that I agree with Jeff. Anyone starting a support group should attend at least four of our group meetings and become trained, and then we will publicize them.

Donna: That would be another option; we can simply tell people we've decided only to put our support groups in our newsletter and on our website, and if they want us to publicize them, they have to be affiliated with us.

Donna stopped her reading and thought, "Okay, there was a clear difference of opinion with at least two members thinking we should publicize established groups and two others who thought they should go through our training, but the conversation seems calm and rational. I summarized our options. What derailed us?" she wondered. She went back to the transcript.

Tina (Healthcare Provider and Latina Board Member): What about agencies that offer support groups for African American and Latina community members? From what I have seen, our organization does not cater to these clients, and they are underserved to begin with, so it would seem part of our mission to provide them with resources.

Eric: I'm a little bit uncomfortable with this idea. Even if we include language on our website that says we're not affiliated with these groups, I think people will still see listing it as an endorsement.

Jeff: Absolutely.

Glenn: It doesn't matter what you do; they will see it that way.

Donna: No, no, not necessarily.

Martin (Caregiver): I don't agree with that. I think you can list our support groups and then have a separate heading that says "other support groups available." It's a way of communicating things that wouldn't be communicated otherwise.

Jeff: But what about the support groups that come and go? What if it is on our website, and someone goes to a meeting, and no one is there, and then they are angry at us?

Eric: Yeah, there has to be some accountability. I don't want to open us up to liability, so we would have to do some screening of who we include.

Donna: I don't want to have to pick and choose. We either have a separate section where we have anybody's support group listed, or we don't put anybody's group in unless it's a Lily Day group. I don't want people sending me e-mails asking me to make exceptions.

Jeff: I don't see how this is our problem. If someone wants information, they go to the Internet, and they can find the programs.

Martin: Or, *or* you call somebody that has that knowledge available to them, and I'd just as soon share what I've learned with others. This is stupid!

Donna stopped reading again and thought, "Yikes, I totally made that conversation about me and what I was willing to do or not do. No wonder Martin got so frustrated. What's worse, we completely ignored Tina's really important observation about supporting minority communities. Eric was making good points about potential legal concerns, which was why we recruited him to the board. Jeff was obviously protecting his program turf, but he also knows the other groups that are out there as well as anyone. Martin and Amanda also raised the importance of making resources available to everyone, which is a critical part of our mission. We never really discussed all the important criteria for making a good decision about this. The usual board members with the loudest voices just kept restating their own concerns while others kept quiet, and I have no idea what they thought."

Donna read through the rest of the transcript and noticed a couple of other interesting aspects of this discussion. There was a long conversation about how they might keep track of other support groups they publicized and whether they were still being offered. The group proposed a couple of ideas: either their newsletter editor could do a periodic follow-up with other groups or the support groups could be responsible for communicating each month that they still wanted to be included in the Lily Day newsletter and website.

After about 20 minutes of coming up with strategies for making sure the information listed was up-to-date, Donna thought they had come to a consensus. She had specifically asked Jeff to make a motion since support groups were a major part of his volunteer efforts for the organization. Donna thought that everyone was taken by surprise when Jeff's motion reverted back to his original position to only include Lily Day support group information on their website and newsletter.

When Donna called for a vote on the motion, there was dead silence. She now realized she should not have asked for a vote since the motion had never been seconded. Following the lack of response to the vote, another board member jumped in and asked Martin if he wanted to offer a motion. Clearly, some board members were seeing this as another conflict between Jeff and Martin. Martin responded by restating his argument that they should publicize all support groups. This led to another long round of conversation, but no motion was ever made.

After another 10 minutes of the meeting went by, Donna became concerned about the need to get to other items on the agenda and asked if they could table the discussion. She was sure that some board members were not happy about this, but they had already spent 40 minutes on this one issue, and they still had not gotten to the discussion of revising the bylaws, which had been on the agenda for months.

Donna began to question her ability to lead this group and realized that despite the fact that the support group conversation seemed to go on forever, it went by so fast that she might never have realized how many important issues were raised. She was also even more nervous about how things were left between Martin and Jeff, as they were frequently at odds with each other, and Jeff may have interpreted Martin's comment as calling him "stupid." It was also awkward that each of them had been specifically asked (by different board members) to make a motion, which reinforced the potential for board divisiveness into a "Martin" and a "Jeff" camp.

Donna made a mental note to contact the university researcher about the possibility of leadership or group facilitation training for herself, and also to look into some board development activities. They needed some intervention to improve their ability to listen to one another and make effective and collaborative decisions for the organization and their clients. More immediately, however, she needed to figure out the best way to reintroduce the question of publicizing non–Lily Day support groups. The bottom line was that Donna needed to have an answer on this so that she could treat all requests for publicity in a consistent manner and move on to the 800 other things on her to-do-list.

KEY TERMS

Interests - the underlying needs and concerns that someone is seeking to meet or address through their stated position.

Parliamentary Procedure - a body of rules used to govern a group meeting. An example of a published set of rules is *Robert's Rules of Order*.

Position - a statement of someone's desired outcome, their preferred solution to a conflict.

Relational Conflict - conflicts that surface because of differences in communication styles or differing expectations of the relationship between parties.

Stakeholders - people who are impacted by the activities of an organization.

Task Conflict - conflicts that surface owing to differences of opinion about how a task should be completed or interpretations of the task itself.

DISCUSSION QUESTIONS

Conflict

1. Was parliamentary procedure the best process for a nonprofit Board of Directors to make this decision? What are its strengths and limitations?
2. What other problem-solving/decision-making processes could have been used?
3. Make a list of all of the positions voiced in this meeting. What are some of the potential interests underlying those positions?

4. What are some possible solutions to the group's problem that would meet all the interests you identified? What may have prevented those alternatives from surfacing in the discussion?

5. What can groups do to prevent relational conflict from turning into task conflict that disrupts effective decision making by a volunteer Board of Directors?

6. When conflict is accompanied by strong emotion, members may use language that derails the board meeting. How might a facilitator or group leader restate the issue to keep the group on track?

Diversity and Participation

7. Discuss the different stakeholders who have an interest in the board's decision about publicizing support groups.

8. How can board members create norms of inclusion and openness to new ideas so that all members believe their contributions are valued?

9. How might a board member orientation be designed to improve meeting participation among new members?

10. What process could be used to prevent domination of meetings by just a few board members of a nonprofit organization?

11. What recommendations would you give Donna for raising the topic of promoting non–Lily Day support groups at the next board meeting?

SUGGESTED READINGS

Bradshaw, P., & Fredette, C. (2011, Spring). The inclusive nonprofit boardroom: Leveraging the transformative potential of diversity. *Nonprofit Quarterly*. Retrieved from https://nonprofitquarterly.org/governancevoice/21570-the-inclusive-nonprofit-boardroomleveraging-the-transformative-potential-of-diversity.html

Cochran, A. C. (2004). *Roberta's rules of order: Sail through meetings for stellar results without the gavel: A guide for nonprofits and other teams.* San Francisco, CA: Jossey-Bass.

Sebenius, J. K. (2005, July). What divides you may unite you. *Negotiation*, 3–5.

Weitzel, A., & Geist, P. (1998). Parliamentary procedure in a community group: Communication and vigilant decision making, *Communication Monographs, 65*, 244–259. doi: 10.1080/03637759809376450

KEYWORDS

diversity, conflict, consensus, parliamentary procedure, Board of Directors

*This case study is based on research conducted with a nonprofit organization over a one-year period. The interaction depicted is drawn from communication in one meeting, although some details have been altered for clarity and educational purposes. The name and mission of the organization have been changed to preserve anonymity.

CHAPTER FOURTEEN

The Choice*

MICHAEL W. KRAMER

University of Oklahoma

Chris had never been in this position before as the president of the Board of Directors of Middleton Community Choir (MCC). Previously, most decisions seemed pretty mundane. The board voted on the concert schedule, which amounted to picking two dates. In a college town, that meant not picking a home football Saturday in the fall and avoiding Easter, Spring Break, Mother's Day, and graduation in the spring. The most controversial decision they made up until now was raising dues for volunteer singers from $10 to $20 to cover increasing costs of music. Even that decision was approved unanimously after some discussion, or at least without any of the eight members voicing disagreement when they voted. The board regularly discussed how to get more than 20–30 singers and more than 100 audience members to a concert. They agreed that was the problem, but no one had any solutions.

This meeting was different. After the founding director, Jonathan, "retired" and moved away, the board needed to select a new director. They invited two respected local directors to interview for the position and present their ideas for MCC. They also had each conduct the choir briefly. Then they planned to vote on "hiring" one of them as the next volunteer director.

Aaron, the first director they interviewed, was well known in the community as the high school choir director. He was capable and confident. He was known for getting a lot out of choirs. His high school choir always received excellent marks in state competitions. His interview went smoothly. His answers to their questions were consistent with the choir's history. For example, longtime board member Carol asked, "What kind of music would you pick?"

Aaron replied, "I'd continue to select a variety of music like you've performed in the past. I enjoyed last spring's concert. It had some classical music like Bach, along with contemporary sacred music like Rutter. It mixed various music styles like jazz and musical show tunes. I think everyone in the audience found something they liked."

A newer board member, Vivian, asked, "What would you do to increase the size of the choir and the audience? It seems a shame to put so much work into our concerts and only about 75 people show up."

"I think there's great potential for growth," Aaron responded. "The most important thing to do is to take advantage of our current members to recruit new members. To increase the audience, we can try two main strategies. First, we could 'check out' a few tickets to each singer, say, 10 or 15, and sort of expect them to sell them. If half of them reach that goal, we'll have 200 people. Then I think we can update our webpage to help advertise our concerts and draw attention to our group. That'll probably bring in more singers, too."

The interview continued along those lines. The practice rehearsal also went smoothly. The choir easily adapted to Aaron's style. Even during the short rehearsal, he seemed to improve their singing.

The board members clearly agreed Aaron would maintain MCC and the singing quality would improve as well. Even though they loved Jonathan, everyone recognized he had somewhat limited skills; by contrast, Aaron was quite skilled. The choir would continue to serve the singers and its loyal audience members, mostly family and close friends. And if some of Aaron's former students joined, the choir and concert attendance would grow. The whole board seemed quite satisfied with Aaron and might have offered him the position on the spot except they had another interview scheduled.

The second director interviewed was Nathan, a noticeably more eccentric individual, who directed three choirs at the town's large Protestant church. The board was surprised by the answer they got when Carol asked him the same question about music.

"The way to make MCC an important part of this community is to create a brand for the choir by doing major works. I would have us perform works like Karl Orff's *Carmina Burana* and Mendelssohn's *Elijah*. Once we start doing the great works of choral music, we'll attract large audiences."

"I don't think we have the talent to perform that music," new board member Samantha replied.

Without hesitation, Nathan responded, "When we advertise the new season and people know we're doing serious music, we'll get all kinds of new members."

Vivian asked, "How will we advertise?"

"We can do the usual things, have members ask others to join and put it on our webpage, which needs a new face, by the way. But I'll also use my network of church choir directors to get the word out."

Quite skeptical, Carol stated, as a matter of indisputable fact, "We don't have the talent to sing the solos. We have people who can do a rousing solo from a musical like *Oklahoma*, but we don't have talent to sing music like that. Those are challenging solos."

"We'll hire soloists. Each great work needs four soloists, a soprano, alto, tenor, and bass. With my university contacts, we'll find people, students or faculty members, eager to perform with us."

"But we've never done that before—hired soloists," responded Carol. "We're a community choir. The soloists should be from the community, not outsiders."

"They'll be from our community. The university is part of our community. And reaching out to the university will attract new singers who haven't heard of MCC. Together we'll be able to perform major works, beginning with Handel's *The Messiah*."

There was a collective gasp when Nathan mentioned *The Messiah*. MCC always thought that performing it would mean they had truly arrived as a community choir, but it never seemed possible. In fact, Carol reminded Nathan, "We don't have an orchestra. We can't perform with just a piano."

"Of course not. Remember, Handel originally had a chamber orchestra and 16 singers," Nathan responded. "I've started a community orchestra this semester, just a small group of 15–20 musicians. When I asked about doing *The Messiah*, they each knew other musicians who would be excited to perform. I know you are concerned about attracting an audience. With the extra 30–40 musicians and more choir members, that would double the audience and then we will double it again by performing *The Messiah* in December when everyone wants to hear it."

"What about money? How can we pay soloists, buy music, and pay the orchestra, too?" asked James, the board treasurer. He was always very practical.

"The larger audience will pay for that."

"But we have to pay for the music up front," James interrupted. "There's not enough money in the treasury for that."

"I know this will be a challenge, but we'll need to raise membership dues to probably $40, but we make it voluntary instead of mandatory. We encourage people to give more than $40 if they can and ask the others to give as much as they can. Over a semester, an extra $20 is like a cup of coffee a week."

And so the interview went. Each time a board member raised an objection, Nathan had a quick reply for how they could overcome that problem.

His rehearsal with the group went quite differently, too. His enthusiasm and sense of humor were contagious. The choir seemed to enjoy themselves like never before, or at least most of them. By the end of the interview, most board members were caught up in the excitement of Nathan's idea for a new and improved MCC. They might have offered him the job on the spot, too.

That was a week ago. Since then, board members had time to step away from the excitement of the moment and consider the issues carefully. The choir members gave them feedback, too. At tonight's meeting, the discussion was quite lively. After some preliminary business, Chris brought up the main agenda item—to which director should they offer the position? Chris tried to be diplomatic in presenting the choice.

"We have two very different options here. If we select Aaron, we will improve in quality and probably grow some. Over time, we may be able to become better known in the community and maintain the spirit of Jonathan and the founding members. If we select Nathan, we'll experience a lot of change. We'll perform different kinds of music accompanied by an orchestra instead of a piano. We'll likely attract a lot more attention than in the past if we manage to pull it off."

After agreeing that those were the issues, people began lining up behind one candidate over the other. Carol articulated her opinion clearly. "We've never hired people to sing with us before. I don't like the idea at all. A community choir should be made up of volunteers, not hired guns."

George, a new board member, responded, "We say that there's a 'Town and Gown' relationship between the university and townspeople. Hiring talented singers from the university builds bridges across the community; it'll make us a community choir of the larger community."

Board members discussed whether or not hiring soloists was appropriate, but then James brought up some financial concerns. "I've run some numbers, and it's true that if we average $40 per choir member and we gain 10 extra singers, we can afford to rent the orchestra music and buy librettos for the singers, but what if that doesn't happen? What if the increase means we lose members? Then we're in the hole, and we can't print money and we can't borrow any either. It's a risky step."

Vivian responded, "I think I can find someone who will promise to cover the difference if we don't break even. I have a friend who was so excited when he heard we might do *The Messiah* that he asked if he could make a donation to MCC. We've never asked for donations before. I bet he'd cover it or at least most of it."

James responded curtly, "It's one thing to say you'll pay for something and another to write the check."

After discussing the economics for a while, Erich, one of MCC's founders, changed the subject to the feedback from current choir members. He noted, "The feedback from choir members was all positive for Aaron, nothing negative. Everyone said he'd improve the quality of our performances. They liked his directing style and personality. The feedback for Nathan was more mixed. Most said Nathan would bring a new energy to the choir that would really make it grow, but a few had really negative things to say, such as that Nathan joked too much and was not serious enough. Others complained that he wanted to change too many things; it made them uncomfortable. I predict we'll lose some current members if we pick him."

"But we lose some singers every year," chimed in Samantha. "That's why we always have to recruit new ones."

"Jonathan always complained about that," added James.

Samantha continued. "Maybe they'll be coming out of the woodwork when they hear we're doing *The Messiah*. And the connection to the university has got to increase our numbers. Maybe we'll lose a few, but I bet we'll gain even more."

Even after a long discussion, there was disagreement on how to evaluate the feedback from current choir members. Vivian turned to the topic of music choice. She commented, "We've always dreamed of doing *The Messiah*. How can we pass up an opportunity to try?"

"But if we can't do it well, I don't want to be part of that. Maybe after Aaron has improved our quality, we'll be ready for it without hiring outside soloists."

And so the discussion went round and round, bringing up topics again and again as the issues often seemed related. Chris recognized that instead of gradually coming to a consensus like at most meetings, the board was becoming more polarized. The discussion lasted much longer than usual. When the meeting had already lasted an hour overtime and it did not seem as if the two sides were any closer to a consensus, he called for a vote. He insisted on a secret ballot so no one was intimidated. Of course, it was quite clear how six of the eight board members would vote: Carol, James, and Erich, all long-term board members, clearly favored Aaron, while Vivian, George, and Samantha, all favored Nathan. That left Jill and Ryan. They both had been on the board for a few years and were used to the way MCC did things. Chris thought those two would cast the deciding votes.

When he counted ballots, Chris was stunned. It was a tie vote, four to four. Now as chair, he had to cast the deciding vote. Should he suggest trying again at the next meeting? They had already announced they would decide this evening. If he cast his vote, what direction would be best for MCC?

KEY TERMS

Institutional Leader - leading by embodying the current values and norms of an organization and communicating to maintain them.

Transactional Leader - managing and maintaining an organization through transactions and communication exchanges with subordinates.

Transformational Leader - leading by creating a vision of change and implementing it through communication with organizational members.

DISCUSSION QUESTIONS

Leadership

1. What characteristics of transactional leaders do Aaron and Nathan exhibit?
2. What characteristics of transformational leaders do Aaron and Nathan exhibit?
3. What characteristics of institutional leaders do Aaron and Nathan exhibit?
4. When type of leadership does a volunteer organization like MCC need in its new director?

Decision Making

5. Did the board clarify the issues, discuss criteria, and analyze the positive and negative outcomes of the decision?
6. What are some limitations to rational decision making models?
7. Is majority rule the best way to make this decision?

General Leadership in Nonprofit Organizations

8. What is the Board of Directors' role in volunteer/nonprofit organizations?
9. What is the director/CEO's role in determining the direction of a volunteer/nonprofit organization?
10. What role should volunteers' feedback have in decision making in volunteer/nonprofit organizations?
11. After Chris casts the deciding vote, what is his responsibility as board president in leading the organization?

SUGGESTED READINGS

Hirokawa, R. Y., & Rost, K. M. (1992). Effective group decision making in organizations: Field test of the vigilant interaction theory. *Management Communication Quarterly, 5,* 267–288. doi: 10.1177/0893318992005003001

Trice, H. M., & Beyer, J. M. (1993). Leadership and organizational cultures. In *The cultures of work organizations* (pp. 254–298). Englewood Cliffs, NY: Prentice Hall.

KEYWORDS

transactional leadership, transformational leadership, institutional leadership, decision making, volunteer Board of Directors

*This case study is based on research conducted on two community choirs that has led to a series of articles in *JACR, CM, WJC, MCQ,* and *Volunteering and Communication: Studies in Multiple Contexts.* The specific data for this case study came from interviews of the two choirs' directors in which they described very different views of their roles when they became directors of their respective choirs.

CHAPTER FIFTEEN

To Participate OR Not TO Participate

Parents, Teachers, and Students in a Geographically Dispersed High School*

MICHELLE T. VIOLANTI

University of Tennessee

Hunter and gold flanked the stairs of an old center-city train station that had been converted into a high school for students interested in science, technology, engineering, and mathematics (STEM). Planning that began years earlier brought state and local officials, parents of newly admitted students, donors, and the press together to welcome the first incoming class of teachers and students. Unlike other public magnet schools, this one drew students from all over the district as well as regional students from surrounding counties. Classmates who lived up to 50 minutes away from one another now shared a classroom. The sheer radius of the school's outreach created challenges for teachers trying to handle the diversities of experience that students brought to the classroom; however, it created even greater challenges for a volunteer-based PTSA (Parent Teacher Student Association) designed to support the school's educational mission.

Less than Six months before the ribbon-cutting ceremony, the first students were admitted, and a group of parents attempted to form a PTSA. They came with little to no background in how to form the organization, recruit volunteers, encourage participation, and/or build relationships with the "local" community. The first parent meeting contained fewer parents than there were slots to fill on the PTSA's executive board and board of managers. Anyone who was willing to serve was given a position with the most critical ones being filled first: president,

president-elect, treasurer, membership, teacher liaison, and fundraising. Initially, the PTSA obtained nonprofit status. With no paid board members, they sought the path of least resistance: find bylaws from other PTSAs that could be easily modified. Bylaws described the organization, its mission, meeting and committee structures, and parliamentary procedures that would govern the meetings.

In the first year, the PTSA succeeded in providing a donation dinner for about 200 students and their families, conducting a T-shirt design contest for their main fundraiser, and hosting a spaghetti dinner/bingo night fundraiser. For the most part, the organization flew under the radar screen of most parents and students because there were few mechanisms for communication. Most activities were planned at the last minute and poorly publicized. During the bingo night fundraiser, the PTSA put forward a ballot for the upcoming year. There were many openings because parents were not volunteering to help what they perceived as a nonexistent organization. At the fundraising dinner, incoming PTSA president Garrett introduced himself to Mabel, a parent in attendance. Mabel responded, "I didn't know there was a PTSA this year. What did you do?" Garrett seemed surprised that Mabel had not checked the PTSA webpage and asked her to become more involved by taking a position for the upcoming year. As the first year ended, the new board vowed to communicate more effectively with PTSA members and become a more integrated part of the school.

The school's second year brought an incoming class that almost outnumbered the sophomores and juniors combined. As an organization, PTSA expected these new families to be as committed to the school and its success as those in the previous year. Those first students came to the school because they were committed to attending a STEM magnet school, and their parents were committed to seeing a new school succeed. Subsequent students came for a variety of reasons, including commitment to a STEM education, a way to escape from an underperforming zoned school, a chance to receive an iPad as part of a technology school, a smaller environment where they would receive more individualized attention, and other parent-driven reasons.

With a change in students also came a change in parents and teachers. Some teachers left because they realized they were not comfortable teaching in a technology-intensive school, some left because they were cherry-picked away by other schools that could pay more, and some left to become administrative coordinators for their various specialties. Each year brought more single parents, more economically disadvantaged families, and more families commuting farther to attend school.

In year two, PTSA memberships increased but not proportionally to the larger number of students. It again hosted its annual donation dinner at the school's open house where parents met their child's teachers, began a practice of giving to the local food pantry and animal shelter, hosted open houses for prospective students, submitted student entries to artistic and written enrichment competitions, helped support teacher training to allow additional advanced placement courses to be offered, and supported student travel for regional and national competitions after they won at the local level. Once again, the student design T-shirt contest and fundraiser were successful, and the PTSA was able to garner parental donations for teacher appreciation meals.

At the end of the second year, new officers were again elected, and the new board developed priorities for year three:

1. Fund a college scholarship for someone in the first graduating class.
2. Develop a membership campaign to increase memberships and retain all teachers as members.
3. Host a program at the school where families are not asked to buy or donate something.
4. Improve communication with the membership, students, and families.
5. Seek opportunities to engage in activities or fund materials to benefit a larger proportion of the student body.

Membership drives coincided with the beginning of school. At the budget meeting, President Katie commented, "I think we should guarantee all our teachers and staff are members this year by buying their memberships."

Treasurer Mabel asked the budget committee, "Is everyone comfortable devoting almost $350 to these memberships?" After some discussion, the board decided to create goodwill by purchasing teacher memberships and save teachers $7.00 each.

During the October board meeting, teacher liaison Rachel revisited the teacher membership issue. "We would likely have been able to sell many of those teacher memberships, and that would have given us more money for planning programs," she said. "While I think the teachers appreciate free memberships, they also don't seem to know that PTSA has helped them in so many ways. When they paid for their memberships, they knew more about what was going on and helped support PTSA." The board continued to discuss the pros and cons of offering complimentary memberships. Most agreed that the teachers were less committed to the PTSA because they did not choose to be members. Peri, who was in charge of hospitality, agreed: "We had fewer teachers attend our open house and parent conference dinners than last year."

Even having purchased memberships for all of the teachers, there were fewer total memberships than the previous year. While the student body increased by over 160, PTSA membership actually decreased by about 30. The board wondered if the decreased interest was a function of not getting the membership message out effectively, depending on high school students to deliver membership forms to their parents, more economically disadvantaged school families, a lack of interest in or knowledge about PTSA, and/or less commitment to the school. The board's second priority was communication. In a board meeting, Mabel had summarized what everyone knew: "No matter where you are, people are on their phones texting, checking the Internet, their mail, and sometimes even talking to another human being. We all know current high school students are part of the digital generation. However, PTSA had never put that technology to work for us." Mabel and others vowed to increase PTSA's online presence, hoping to better connect with both member and students. In year three, PTSA got its own link on the school's webpage, developed a Facebook page, and solicited Twitter followers.

Even with the new technologies, communication was still a challenge. Privacy issues prevented the school from providing contact information and a nonschool personnel member from having access to the website. Therefore, the board's distribution list was based on membership registration forms or people opting in via social media. The board soon learned that even though the students were all digital natives, not all of their parents and grandparents were as digitally savvy or had the desire to communicate electronically.

Membership and communication, however, were not PTSA's only challenges. Fundraising is a double-edged sword in a public school system. While many believed there should be public funds for educational endeavors, legislators, parents, and administrators knew those dollars were never sufficient to provide all of the desired learning opportunities. At the high school level where students are no longer cute elementary students and not as motivated by token prizes, there were fewer fundraising options. In year two, the PTSA sold tumblers, car magnets, and clings with the school logo on them. They still had more leftovers than they would likely sell for many years; they thought like parents rather than students when they created the fundraising options. In contrast, the board was extremely successful with T-shirts because most high school students wanted school apparel at a reasonable price, and parents were often willing to buy it for them. More importantly, a shirt designed by a fellow student increased purchasing.

The board needed someone to coordinate the T-shirt fundraiser, but they soon realized that fundraising was the hardest place to recruit volunteers. Fundraisers are often people who see the big picture but who do not understand the detailed nature of making sure all of the "i"s are dotted and "t"s are crossed for the auditors. There were multiple occasions when the fundraising volunteer threatened to quit because she was asked to provide paperwork for everything ordered and sold. She found it offensive that anyone would question her. Because she was a volunteer giving her time and effort, the treasurer and other board members had to tread lightly until all T-shirts were delivered and the books were audited.

Although the issues of membership, communication, and fundraising were challenging at best, the PTSA board did not want to neglect their role in programming. PTSA held a program for students and their families to attend on one's digital footprint. Three members of the local community discussed the ways college admissions offices, campus organizations, and potential employers use the Internet to trace a person's online history. Board members agreed that at a STEM school where students were online more hours than they slept, this should interest both students and their parents.

While planning the event, members debated about what time the event should occur: "Students leave at 4:30, and some don't get home until 5:30 because of distance from the school. To allow for dinner and coming back to school, we should have it at 7:00 p.m.," said Samantha, the parliamentarian.

"If we have it at 5:00 or 5:30 p.m., students can stay after school and the families can have dinner after the program," responded Chloe, the vice president.

The decision was made to go with 7:00 p.m. to give the speakers time to eat dinner beforehand. Approximately 12–15 families out of the school's 400ish families attended. As the event concluded, Katie had mixed feelings about its success. She wondered, "Was it a success because the PTSA was able to give something to the STEM families without asking them for a donation or to buy something? Or was it a failure because so few people attended?"

At the close of the third year, the PTSA continued to face several challenges.

1. The nominating committee for next year's board was having difficulty filling all of its positions without violating the bylaws that indicated no one could serve in a position for more than two years.
2. The membership committee still needed to address why fewer people were joining each year even as the school grew.
3. The communication committee needed to walk the tightrope between reaching everyone and information overload.
4. The PTSA continued to struggle to attract parents and students to the school for activities that occurred outside school hours.

The school's vision included "inquiry-based instruction challenging students to solve real-world problems and develop critical thinking skills." Katie hoped that each subsequent board would take a page from the school's book and continue to push the traditional boundaries to develop creative solutions to their own real-world problems as a volunteer organization.

KEY TERMS

Culture - values, behaviors, and symbols that indicate how things work in an organizational setting.

Diversity - people with different ethnic, cultural, social, ideological experiences.

Identification - the extent to which individuals align themselves with an organization because they share similar values.

Stakeholders - anyone or any group with an interest in an organization; these people can affect and/or be affected by the organization.

Vision - an aspirational statement about what an organization hopes to achieve.

DISCUSSION QUESTIONS

Building Stakeholder Relationships

1. How do you persuade/motivate/encourage people with long commutes to become organizational members or volunteers?
2. PTSA board members and volunteers never had to deal with a geographically dispersed school. What are some of the unique problems that situation creates? How can they adapt to this situation?

Organizational Identification and Socialization

3. How do you cultivate identification in a geographically dispersed organization?
4. What socialization mechanisms can be used to help people unfamiliar with geographically dispersed organizations?

Organizational Culture

5. How do you create and maintain a culture of participation in school-based activities or programs?
6. Given a school of technology, how should PTSA use technology to communicate with their various stakeholders?

Ethical Considerations

7. Various stakeholders may have different expectations for this school. What might the following stakeholders expect? And how would you handle their varying, and sometimes competing, expectations?
   a. Parents interested in promoting the school

    b. Parents interested in creating the best experience possible for enrolled students

    c. Community members who believe the school should not exist

    d. Universities that hope to recruit these students because they have technology proficiency not available in other state high schools

    e. Faculty and administrators seeking grant opportunities and positive press

8. How do you create a mission and vision that meet the varied needs of the diverse students, parents, and teachers who are current or future members?

SUGGESTED READINGS

Ashforth, B. E., & Mael, F. (1989). Social identity theory and the organization. *Academy of Management Review, 14*, 20–39. doi: 10.5465/AMR.1989.4278999

Balser, D., & McClusky, J. (2005). Managing stakeholder relationships and nonprofit organization effectiveness. *Nonprofit Management & Leadership, 15*, 295–315. doi: 10.1002/nml.70

Boezeman, E. J., & Ellemers, N. (2008). Volunteer recruitment: The role of organizational support and anticipated respect in non-volunteers' attraction to charitable volunteer organizations. *Journal of Applied Psychology, 93*, 1013–1026. doi: 10.1037/0021-9010.93.5.1013

Burnside-Lawry, J. (2012). Listening and participatory communication: A model to assess organization listening competency. *International Journal of Listening, 26*, 102–121. doi: 10.1080/10904018.2012.678092

Gilpin, D. R., & Miller, N. K. (2013). Exploring complex organizational communities: Identity as emergent perceptions, boundaries, and relationships. *Communication Theory, 23*, 148–169. doi: 10.1111/comt.12008

Van Puyvelde, S., Caers, R., DuBois, C., & Jegers, M. (2012). The governance of nonprofit organizations: Integrating agency theory with stakeholder and stewardship theories. *Nonprofit and Voluntary Sector Quarterly, 41*, 431–451. doi: 10.1177/0899764011409757

KEYWORDS

volunteer recruitment, organizational identification, organizational culture, stakeholder communication, relationship building

*These data were collected over three years with the author serving as a parent the first year, PTSA executive board member years two and three, and PTSA member for all three years. The names have all been changed.

Volunteer Experiences: Motivation, Identity, AND Balance

CHAPTER SIXTEEN

Really Helping?

Understanding Volunteerism in a Tornado Relief Effort*

ALAINA C. ZANIN

University of Oklahoma

On May 20, 2013, at 2:56 p.m., Allie sat on the floor in the hallway of her build-ing at the University of Oklahoma. She chatted with her classmates and professor about the readings for their summer leadership seminar amid blaring tornado sirens. Tornado sirens in Oklahoma were relatively common during the months of May and June, desensitizing almost, but today was different. Allie and her classmates began getting weather updates, with newscasters warning residents of Cleveland County to "get underground or get out of the way." As the updates climatically progressed, they learned that an F5 tornado was touching down just 10 miles north of their university in the city of Moore. Allie saw the worry in her classmates' faces. She thought hard. Were any of her friends or family traveling north this afternoon? Could they be in the path of the tornado?

By 3:35 p.m., the tornado warning was lifted. One of the most devastating in the history of the state, this F5 tornado was on the ground for 39 minutes and left a 17-mile-long path of destruction, which included a heavily populated area in Moore, Okay, just a few miles northwest of the university. Allie returned to her apartment to see if she had any damage from the storm. Her apartment was un-touched, just as she had left it. Allie watched as images of the destruction flashed across the television screen in her apartment. Whole subdivisions were flattened—homes erased from the earth. Neighborhoods were replaced with twisted metal, mattresses, clothing, photo albums, and teddy bears strewn over lawns and side-walks. A young news reporter stood outside of what was left of an elementary school. The screen cut to a shot of parents being reunited with their children, hugging and clinging to them, sobbing tears of joy.

As Allie watched, she thought about how narrowly she had missed the tornado's destruction. She thought about how she would be safely sleeping in her bed that night, while hundreds of people in the next town had lost everything, including their loved ones. Given her proximity to destruction, the least she could do would be to help. These people were her neighbors. In the past, Allie had watched slow government bureaucracies respond to natural disasters. She did not want to succumb to the bystander effect by assuming "someone else" would help those people rebuild. She was in a unique position to be able to provide some sort of help on her own, and maybe collectively as well. Some of her classmates had already started posting to social media about ways to get involved through donations and cleanup efforts. The department administrative assistant sent out an e-mail explaining ways in which Oklahomans could give immediate help to other Oklahomans. The Department of Leadership and Volunteerism at the university was already providing emergency housing and meals to 100 victims as well as emergency volunteers. They were allowing students to volunteer in a variety of ways: childcare, cooking/distributing meals, debris cleanup, driving supplies and goods, etcetera.

The next day in class, Allie announced that she had signed up online to volunteer through the Department of Leadership and Volunteerism. Officials were discouraging individuals from "helping" without going through local churches and nonprofit organizations because of safety, liability, and security concerns. There had been a few unverified reports of looting. Also, traffic on the highway had been gridlocked around the Moore exits since the tornado touched down. Several of Allie's classmates coordinated schedules and signed up for four-hour volunteer slots together.

The following day, Allie parked her car in front of the high-rise dorm on campus that was being used as temporary housing for tornado victims. Once inside, she was bombarded by a flurry of activity, small children sprawled out on the floor coloring, while a couple of undergraduates in fraternity shirts carried cases of water bottles downstairs. There were handwritten signs that directed Allie to a table where she signed in under her name, which was neatly printed in an alphabetized list. The woman behind the table said that she had enough volunteers on-site but asked if Allie and her classmates would want to drive up to Moore to help clear debris. Allie and her classmates were excited. This was a *real* opportunity to help. Whether or not they were willing to admit it, they were also curious. The woman explained that they would be representing OU and to follow directions of the coordinator at the Moore Community Center. Each of them plastered a temporary name tag to their OU shirts and jumped in the car to head north to Moore.

The drive to Moore usually took 15 minutes; however, given the influx of rescue personal and gawkers from the interstate, Allie finally pulled into the Moore

Community Center gravel parking lot an hour later. Allie and her classmates checked in at another table and were told by a badly sunburned volunteer to sign a waiver form, take a water bottle, sunscreen, and brand-new work gloves from a nearby bin. The gym had been converted into a makeshift command center, and there were people bustling in and out. Some were chatting, sitting at picnic tables outside, some were coordinating rides, and a few were on cell phones or walkie-talkies giving incoherent directions to someone on the other end. There were a few tables sporadically set up around the gymnasium, and every kind of junk food imaginable had been piled high on top. Every few minutes, a different volunteer would offer a snack or drink to Allie or one of her classmates. Allie was a bit taken aback. She was not the one who needed help; she was the one who was there to help.

Then walkie-talkie man cleared his throat and gathered all of the new volunteers. He explained how grateful he was to see so much support from the community and reminded the volunteers that the cleanup would take a long time. He encouraged the group to come back and keep coming back even after the Moore tornado wasn't the top news headline. Next he explained their plan of action. The disaster area had been mapped into several zones, and each zone had a command tent with a disaster relief coordinator. Allie and her classmates were to carpool to Zone F, meet with the coordinator, pick up any tools they might need, like shovels, and get directions as to which house needed debris cleared.

They piled back into the car with a map of the disaster zones in hand and started to make their way to a residential area that had been devastated by the storm. By this time, Allie had been trying to volunteer for nearly two hours, and she was once again stuck in crawling traffic. In the disaster zone, the mood in the car was somber and silent. The damage up close was worse than Allie had envisioned. They parked near the makeshift command tent, which looked like it was built for tailgating rather than disaster relief. Again, there were four long tables full of hamburgers, pizza, hot dogs, chips, candy, cookies, and granola bars.

Before Allie opened her mouth, one of the volunteers, Daryl, as his name tag indicated, said, "Hi, ladies, would any of you like a snack or bottle of water?"

Allie replied, "No, thank you. We're from the University of Oklahoma Department of Leadership and Volunteerism. We want to help with the cleanup."

The volunteers looked at one another, perplexed.

Daryl said, "Well, I'm not too sure where our zone director ran off to, but y'all can grab them shovels over there and head down the street." He pointed to several damaged houses down the road. He said, "Y'all just pile the debris on the curb, and a truck will be by in the next few days to take it away."

Allie replied, "Thank you. We'll get to work!"

Allie and her classmates took their tools and walked half a mile into the subdivision. Several of the houses had symbols spray painted on their doors demonstrating that they had been cleared and no one was trapped inside. The neighborhood had an eerie and postapocalyptic feeling. On one side of the street, the houses only had minimal damage; some were missing a few shingles or had a downed tree in their yard, while the houses on the other side of the street were gutted with their interior walls exposed for onlookers. Allie and her classmates chose a house to start working on. The garage had collapsed on a car, and several of the bricks had to be removed. Allie felt a little torn about working on this house. The homeowners were not home. They did not have permission to be on their property.

Allie and her classmates worked quietly clearing bricks, splinters of wood, insulation, pictures, dish towels, a baby bottle, and broken glasses. Four different times, work crews in matching T-shirts riding in the backs of trucks drove past and asked if Allie needed help, food, or water. She declined each time. Allie was picking up debris in the side yard of the house and encountered the neighboring homeowner.

She asked, "Sir, do you need any help clearing some of that debris off of your lawn?"

He looked at her suspiciously. He replied in a curt tone, "No, thank you," and turned his back to Allie.

Allie said, "Okay, just let me know if you change your mind."

He spun back around and said, "This house is totaled. There is nothing here for you to do. I just want my insurance money and to be done with it."

Allie's eyes filled with tears, and she replied meekly, "I'm sorry. I didn't mean to bother you."

She returned to her classmates.

One of her classmates, Veronica, said, "I'm really sorry guys, but I have so much work to do for class tomorrow. I wasn't anticipating this taking so long. Do y'all care if we head back? I think traffic is going to be just as bad getting out of here."

Allie did not want to hold up the group. She said, "Yeah, I'm ready, I guess."

Veronica said, "Don't worry, Allie. We can come back in the next couple days. There will still be a ton of cleanup going on. We helped out enough for today."

Allie wanted to return to Moore the next day as well, but she was beginning to question how much help she was actually providing. She was frustrated by how the day had gone. She had spent more time driving around trying to help than actually *helping*. Once they arrived in the disaster zone and started digging into the *real work* of clearing debris, they had made little progress in the hour or so they were there. To top it off, Allie's one encounter with an actual tornado victim demonstrated that her futile attempts to help were not necessarily having an impact.

On the ride home, Allie also felt a sense of guilt. What were her real motivations for wanting to help? Were they truly altruistic or were they somewhat self-motivated? Was her pitch to her classmates to volunteer just an attempt to feel better or feel helpful as opposed to helpless? Was helping a type of catharsis? Was it because she wanted a sense of control over the situation? She was worried, too, that her motivations for going might have stemmed from her curiosity and the media sensationalism of the event, rather than from selflessness. Would it be unethical for her to post pictures to social media about helping? Allie could tell herself that she was promoting the cause and influencing others to help as well, but wasn't she also framing her own identity as philanthropic? Was she being selfish and disingenuous? Especially given that she was not so sure her "help" was even helpful. Allie felt deflated as they drove south. She wrestled with these questions and whether or not she should return the next day.

KEY TERMS

Discursive Construction - the creation of social reality through communicative interaction.

Framing - the process of communicating a specific mental picture to others.

Philanthropic Identity - a self-concept in which individuals view themselves as "doers of good work."

Sensemaking - the ongoing retrospective development of plausible images that rationalize what people do through social interaction.

DISCUSSION QUESTIONS

Volunteering and Identity (Mize Smith, 2013; Winterich, Mittal, Swartz, & Aquino, 2013)

1. Why is Allie struggling to claim a philanthropic identity?
2. In what ways is Allie's philanthropic identity central and/or emerging?
3. How do the rules and resources afforded to the volunteers influence the construction of philanthropic identities?
4. How does the phenomenon of volunteers helping volunteers relate to philanthropic identity construction?

Framing and Sensemaking (Fairhurst, 2011; Maitlis & Lawrence, 2007; Weick, 1995)

5. How do volunteers discursively construct what *helping* is?
6. How do volunteers discursively construct *who* needs help?

Volunteer Motivation and Organizational Barriers (Bidee et al., 2013)

7. How do interpersonal interactions impact a volunteer's experience and what it means to help?

8. What are some factors that motivate volunteers to help with disaster relief?

9. How many/much of a volunteer organization's resources should be used to help volunteers?

10. What are some barriers (e.g., discursive, organizational, environmental, personal) to volunteering?

11. As a competent communicator, what are some recommendations you would give leaders in the nonprofit organizations in this case to increase volunteer motivation and to reduce volunteer turnover?

12. How should Allie ethically proceed in her volunteering efforts?

SUGGESTED READINGS

Bidee, J., Vantilborgh, T., Pepermans, R., Huybrechts, G., Willems, J., Jegers, M., & Hofmans, J. (2013). Autonomous motivation stimulates volunteers' work effort: A self-determination theory approach to volunteerism. *Voluntas: International Journal of Voluntary & Nonprofit Organizations, 24*(1), 32–47. doi: 10.1007/s11266-012-9269-x

Fairhurst, G. T. (2011). *The power of framing: Creating the language of leadership.* San Francisco, CA: Jossey-Bass.

Maitlis, S., & Lawrence, T. B. (2007). Triggers and enablers of sensegiving in organizations. *Academy of Management Journal, 50*(1), 57–84. doi: 10.5465/AMJ.2007.24160971

Mize Smith, J. (2013). Volunteer tourists: The identity and discourse of travelers combining largesse and leisure. In M. W. Kramer, L. K. Lewis, & L. M. Gossett (Eds.), *Volunteering and communication: Studies from multiple contexts* (pp. 189–212). New York, NY: Peter Lang.

Weick, K. E. (1995). *Sensemaking in organizations.* Thousand Oaks, CA: Sage.

Winterich, K. P., Mittal, V., Swartz, R., & Aquino, K. (2013). When moral identity symbolization motivates prosocial behavior: The role of recognition and moral identity internalization. *Journal of Applied Psychology, 98*, 759–770. doi: 10.1037/a0033177

KEYWORDS

philanthropic identity, sensemaking, framing, volunteer motivation

*This case study is based on a first-person ethnographic account of the author's volunteer experience during the Moore tornado recovery effort. This case study was written as an extension of the author's field notes of the event. In writing this account, the author also solicited feedback from colleagues who participated as volunteers.

CHAPTER SEVENTEEN

Facing Identity Questions during Organizational Change*

MURRAY W. LEE AND JANE STUART BAKER

University of Alabama

John and Sara had attended First Church every Sunday for decades. Their wedding, and later that of their child, their parents' funerals—all had taken place there. Not only did the church represent important milestones in their lives, but the pastor was also important to them, as he had been present at each of these significant life events. So when the pastor retired, John and Sara wondered, "What will the new leader be like? Will this be the same church?" The arrival of the new pastor confirmed their worst fears: change was coming. After months of struggle with new church leadership, John and Sara left First Church, along with many others. An organization that had thrived for years was now facing serious questions about its future.

Sara and John were just arriving home from the Sunday service at their new church. "I miss First Church." Sara sighed. "We worked so hard to help make the church what it is. It's where we belong. Why did it have to change?"

John and Sara plopped down on the sofa in their inviting living room. They turned to look at the gallery of photographs on the wall behind them—framed black-and-white images taken during years of mission trips with First Church, a beautiful mosaic of happy moments spent in service to those in need. As they studied the photographs, they reflected on their time at the church, trying to make sense of all that had changed.

John and Sara felt as if they were key members of the church even though the congregation was nearly 1,500 members. "It's *our* church," they would say. Many of the ideals that First Church held so dearly seemed to align with John and Sara's own passions: a love for missions, compassion for those who were less financially capable, and ministry beyond the immediate community. John and Sara sought to nurture these values in the church.

The home page of First Church's website bore its mission statement: "First Church is a Christian, mission-focused church whose purpose is to glorify God by reaching up in worship, reaching in for discipleship, and reaching out in compassion." It was John's marketing firm that had helped develop the statement so many years prior.

Of all the values and ministries that First Church represented, it was the focus on Christian mission outreach that most captured John's and Sara's hearts. For years John and Sara participated in church missions through travel, prayer, and fundraising efforts. They felt so drawn to mission outreach that they quickly found a place to serve on the Missions Committee. While First Church was located in the Southeast United States, their personal love for New England became a focus for resources and trips. John would often remind the committee, "Our heart lies in seeing pastors in the Northeast build quality relationships with their communities. This is where Sara and I grew up, and it's still where we spend our vacations and our money."

First Church's senior pastor, Reverend Wilson, was always supportive. "If this is important to you, Sara and John, this is important to First," he would say. He didn't just say those kinds of things in private either. There were regular ministry announcements from the pulpit on Sunday mornings: "This morning we are going to pray for Reverend Smith and his family, who are serving in Connecticut, and take up a special offering for them. Their church, though well-meaning, is not able to pay his salary, and we can't have his three children going hungry."

The outpouring of love and support by the congregation was huge. One member once remarked to Sara, "I can recall that Sunday so vividly. We collected $23,000 that day! I watched as my own nine-year-old son gave every last penny in his piggy bank for the Smiths' special offering. I've never felt more strongly that I was part of something bigger than myself than at that moment."

John and Sara often spoke fondly of their first experience on a mission trip, which was a home repair project for elderly residents in Maine. "When we went to Maine with that first team and saw the differences that God was making in people's lives, we felt led to encourage other church members to share their gifts of service as well. That's why we took teams of people every year for six years!"

That first trip turned out to be self-defining for one young woman, Cassidy, who accompanied the team. Cassidy felt a little intimidated when John and Sara first urged her to go. She said, "What do I possibly have to contribute? I am not a builder. I've never hammered a nail in my life!" Soon Cassidy's insecurities gave way to a deep passion for helping those in need. She earned a bachelor's degree in community development and moved to Maine after college to work with a local community center. "I couldn't have done any of this without John and Sara," she gushed. No one ever knew that John and Sara also paid for her entire trip that first year, as well as support, her financially after college for her first three years in Maine.

Despite the fulfillment John and Sara felt from their involvement with the Missions Committee, their experience at First Church was not completely rosy. Although John could be deeply giving, he was also a sarcastic man who would often use his quick wit and superior intelligence to get what he wanted. Some members of the Missions Committee, though grateful for the years of sacrifice from John and Sara, had grown tired of the strong-arming. Jessica and Michael, recent members who were born and raised in the local community and now had their own young family, represented this growing faction. During one committee meeting, Jessica remarked, "Is New England the *only* focus of this church?"

John knew how to keep his cool and replied in the same way he usually did in moments like this. "Of course it isn't the only focus," he quipped with a sly grin. "It's just the most important one."

"Sometimes," Michael added, "I wonder why we give so many of our resources to helping out up there when there's so much need right here in our own backyard! Sometimes I think, as well-intentioned as we are, that we are totally out of touch with the needs that are right here around us!"

John and Sara weren't fazed. They remembered what Reverend Wilson had told them time and time again. The ministry about which they were so passionate mattered. His words echoed in their ears, drowning out Jessica and Michael's critical outbursts.

Despite John's slick talk, some long-standing members and newcomers like Jessica and Michael were beginning to agree that the church should place less emphasis on New England missions, though to what degree was a matter of debate. The church's shifting priorities really came to a head when, after three decades of service, Reverend Wilson retired for health reasons, and a new pastor replaced him. His replacement, Reverend Hill, was, in John's words, "a significant obstacle" to New England missions at First Church. Reverend Hill was young and somewhat inexperienced, and, although he valued missions, he felt the focus needed to change. Unfortunately, he was unable to communicate his case in a compassionate way.

During a private meeting one day with Sara and John, he blurted out, "I appreciate all the years of service this church has given to the northeastern US, John, but it's a new day at First Church, and we just can't keep pouring resources into an area where we get no bang for our buck."

"What are you talking about?" screamed Sara in response. "No bang for our buck? That's the most crass thing I've ever heard. Don't you realize all of the blood, sweat, and tears the Missions Committee has poured into projects in New England? If you're not careful, we'll leave and take our time—*and money*—to a church that actually shares our values!"

It wasn't long before Sara's threat became a reality. When she and John sensed that First Church was moving away from an emphasis on New England missions, they decided to leave. John and Sara visited an array of different churches, hoping to find one that prioritized missions in exactly the way that aligned with their own ideals.

John and Sara did not take their decision to leave First Church lightly. Long before they began visiting other churches, they and other concerned church members attempted to bring back the traditional focus. Night after night, John and Sara hosted dinners in their home, made public to any who were interested, seeking to preserve the mission and vision they felt was so important to First Church.

"I don't know, John," said Rick, a fellow member. Have you seen Reverend Hill's vision for missions? It's affordable to the young families of the church, easy to serve because it's local, and the results are so very obvious."

"But we cannot give up on these families!" John replied. He was getting angry now. "They depend on us!"

"No, John, that's where you're wrong. They depend on the Lord. They just use us for our money."

For John, what was more troubling than Rick's words was the fact that Rick was someone who really mattered in the church—a decision-maker, an elder.

At First Church, decisions were made not only by the paid or professional leadership, but also by a core group of laypeople known as elders. Elder rule became a norm for decision making that was difficult to change, and church laws were constructed to ensure its permanence. When the new pastor arrived, he and the elders first decided to make changes to the Sunday morning service, resulting in a more contemporary format. About 50 of the 1,500 members vocalized their disagreement, which only prompted the church elders to tighten their control around the new pastor and staff and in turn become even more resistant to the group's criticism. Eventually the 50 dissenting members opted out and took their money with them, leaving First Church financially strapped. John and Sara were not part of this "angry group," as the dissenters came to be known, because worship style was largely irrelevant to them. However, these events only foreshadowed what was to come: the Missions Committee was about to take a financial hit.

After the "angry group" left the church, the elders faced a predicament—where to make budget cuts. Without consulting John and Sara and others who had spent decades promoting missions, the elders approved a cut of hundreds of thousands of dollars and all of the New England missionaries were summarily dropped. At the same time, the elders hired three new youth staff, in alignment with Reverend Hill's vision for the ever-younger church.

"We have to make cuts in order to survive," explained Rick to John. "And if it's going to be cuts anywhere, it's going to be in areas that are no longer our main focus."

"Not our main focus?" fumed John. "Is this where the church is headed? I can't believe that we're hiring additional staff during a budget cut! When money gets tight, we cut missionaries and add church staff? Let me get this straight; we cut funding for hungry pastors to pay other pastors who aren't necessary for a dwindling church? Forget this!"

John and Sara were outraged. The changes in the worship service, though significant, were not dramatic enough to motivate them to leave. However, cutting the mission budget was the final straw. They had to face the reality; First Church was changing, and there was nothing they could do about it.

The elders at First Church began to label John and Sara as "troublemakers" and "detractors with disruptive ideas." While John and Sara viewed their concerns as legitimate, they voiced them during a season of uncertainty and so aroused suspicion. The elders feared that John and Sara sought to fracture the church, just like the 50 angry members who left.

From that point on, Sara and John were not welcomed into the decision-making circle of the core group of members and elders. The church was in flux. *Who are we? Who are we going to be?* The questions swarmed like angry bees among the remaining members. Through all of this, one question was on John and Sara's minds: *What happened to* our *church?*

KEY TERMS

Change - shifts in the structures or systems of an organization that may challenge its identity and purpose.

Organizational Identification - an individual's sense of connectedness or oneness with an organization.

Organizational Identity - the core elements that make an organization unique and recognizable across time.

DISCUSSION QUESTIONS

1. How would you characterize First Church's identity as an organization both before and after the change in leadership?
2. How can we understand John's and Sara's individual identities and First Church's organizational identity in light of one another?
3. How do people come to identify with certain organizations and not others?

4. Under what conditions might people lose their sense of identification with a particular nonprofit organization?
5. Why did Sara and John lack the ability to maintain the influence they once had?
6. When members leave a church or other voluntary organization, what kinds of organizational identity questions might face those who choose to stay?
7. Albert and Whetten (1985) have explained that an organization's identity can be understood by its "central, distinct, and enduring" elements. What challenges does this case present when considering this definition?

SUGGESTED READINGS

Albert, S. A., & Whetten, D. A. (1985). Organizational identity. In L. L. Cummings & B. M. Staw (Eds.), *Research in organizational behavior* (Vol. 7, pp. 263-295). Greenwich, CT: JAI Press.

Cheney, G., & Tompkins, P. K. (1987). Coming to terms with organizational identification and commitment. *Central States Speech Journal, 38*, 1-15. doi: 10.1080/10510978709368225

McNamee, L. G. (2011). Faith-based organizational communication and its implications for member identity. *Journal of Applied Communication Research, 39*, 422-440. doi: 10.1080/00909882.2011.608697

Meisenbach, R. J., & Kramer, M. (2014). Exploring nested identities: Voluntary membership, social category identity, and identification in a community choir. *Management Communication Quarterly, 28*, 187-213. doi: 10.1177/0893318914524059

Scott, C. R. (2007). Communication and social identity theory: Existing and potential connections in organizational identification research. *Communication Studies, 58*, 123-138. doi: 10.1080/10510970701341063

Williams, E. A., & Connaughton, S. L. (2012). Expressions of identifications: The nature of talk and identity tensions among organizational members in a struggling organization. *Communication Studies, 63*, 457-481. doi: 10.1080/10510974.2011.630439

KEYWORDS

organizational identity, organizational identification, leadership succession, change

*This case follows a series of events that unfolded in a church in the midst of leadership transition. As the senior pastor of a church in the same city, the first author witnessed the transition firsthand and applied a variety of organizational and communication theories to explain why the church lost members who found themselves and the church they loved so dearly in the midst of an identity crisis.

CHAPTER EIGHTEEN

Communicating Commitment

Volunteer Retention at Parents First*

KIRSTIE McALLUM

Université de Montréal

Alison intended to take advantage of her flextime at the Department of Health and leave the office half an hour early to finish the brochure about the new coffee group before the evening's meeting. However, she was stopped in her tracks by a conversation at the photocopier.

"Parents First does a great job with the medical checkups for kids under five years old, but I don't understand why the clinic looks so shabby. It needs a new coat of paint," complained her colleague Dan.

"Really, Dan, you should put your money where your mouth is and make a donation," Alison suggested. "It's a nonprofit organization, after all. The government pays the nurses' salaries, but since 1907, volunteers have taken on everything else! We only have six active members, all mothers in their late 20s and early 30s, who do it all: finance the building and upkeep of the clinics, fundraise for parent education courses, and organize playgroups for children and support groups for moms." Alison left the building with a sizable check for the volunteer committee's next project.

Creating Space to Volunteer

As Fiona raced around the kitchen, putting the last ingredients into the spaghetti sauce and pulling the salad out of the fridge, she reflected that although volunteering for Parents First helped her avoid mommy brain, it certainly increased her workload. One Tuesday night a month, she transformed into superwoman, ensuring the dinner was cooked (and even better than usual), the kids bathed, and the house spotless. Little surprise that she would arrive at the meeting late and a little frazzled. "I hope we're not going to work on our business plan tonight," she said as she slipped on her coat.

Tim stepped into the hallway and put his hand on her shoulder: "You don't *have* to do this, Fiona. What are they going to do? Sack you? You're only a volunteer. You could stop all of this if you wanted to."

Fiona smiled. "Yes, I know. I'll be home soon."

Tim snorted. "Hmmph. You and your girlfriends will be gasbagging for hours!"

Five streets away, Emma was trying to extricate herself from a phone conversation with the president of the Parent Teacher Association. "Sorry, Edith, but I've got a meeting tonight to plan the next round of fundraising for the baby massage courses. I've really got to go."

Edith paused for a moment and then commented, "You know that you're mad. Can't someone else run the meetings for you now and again? Someone who doesn't have three kids to look after?"

Emma struggled to restrain her irritation. "No, not really. It's not that easy to find someone willing to take on responsibility. You can't just jump on people and say, 'Hey! I don't want to do this anymore. Can you do it?' People are just—'Why don't you want to do it? If it's not fun for you, it won't be fun for me either!' Besides, it's not that much work. I do between one and maybe ten hours a week. I mean, this is a busier week, but last week was next to nothing." After she hung up, she thanked her lucky stars that her husband, Jamie, was so supportive. Unlike the horror stories that the rest of the girls shared about their other halves, Jamie never grumbled about the late-night meetings, the constant influx of messages jamming their family e-mail account, or the Saturdays dedicated to baby gear sales and sausage sizzles. In fact, he'd even helped build the clinic's playground two months ago.

Across town, Margie grabbed the committee's accounts off the kitchen table and placed them in her handbag. She was pleased that her partner, David, exhausted after finishing the farm's crop round, had not noticed them. Those accounts had led to one of their biggest fights ever. David had come home with roses and movie tickets to find the accounts spread out over the table and Margie trying to fix mistakes the previous treasurer had made—errors that could lead to accusations of poor accounting and loss of the organization's charity status. With no time to spare before the next meeting, she'd refused to go out. It was partly her sense of responsibility and partly her way of repaying the debt of gratitude she owed to the girls who had looked after her when she'd had postnatal depression after Matthew's birth. When they'd visited, David was always out in the fields. She headed off possible objections to her departure, promising to watch a movie with David on her return and to make cookies with Matthew the next day.

Margie's best friend, Noreen, was stuck in traffic. She had started attending meetings with Margie seven months ago, to get out of the house and do something different. The information session presented Parents First as a family-friendly organization where volunteers determined the time they could commit to community development, given their other responsibilities and interests. "If only it were possible to give just a couple of hours!" she reflected ruefully. "The problem is that the committee is too small for the fundraising we need to do. We all put in so many hours that it's impossible to convince a new volunteer that it's not going to suck up all her free time."

The Meeting

The meeting's official start time was 7:30 p.m. Emma arrived early and clustered the chairs into a semicircle and placed the minutes of the previous meeting on each one. She couldn't wait for the others to arrive. She loved the sense of mutual support that she'd found in the group and the skills that being part of it had developed: running meetings, organizing fundraising events, creating reports, and liaising with other nonprofit organizations and the media. But more than that, the volunteer role expanded her knowledge of her friends. She'd discovered strengths that she would never have noticed if they only interacted during school drop-offs or family picnics. "It's almost like working with them," she concluded. "I've seen a totally different side of my friends, and they've seen a different side of me as well."

The meeting room, adjacent to the nurses' clinic, was welcoming. The furniture was new, the paint fresh, and the kitchenette well-appointed. She arranged her home-baked lemon meringue pie on a plate and sat down to wait. Margie arrived next, feeling slightly uncomfortable about leaving the packet of store cookies that she had hastily picked up on the way on the counter, until Noreen burst through the door with plastic supermarket bags in both hands.

"It's a miracle I'm here!" she announced. "The government should hire me as a negotiator. The amount of bargaining I have to do to get out the door is outrageous. If I go out tonight, then tomorrow night ..."

Margie laughed in agreement. "Tell me about it!" she said.

Emma decided to begin with the first items on the agenda at 7:40, even though attendance was thin. "Okay, we need to figure out who's going to ask the supermarket manager for permission to collect donations, who'll make the signage, and who'll call up people to man the stand."

"Oh, you mean *woman* the stand, don't you?" commented Alison, who pushed open the door with Fiona right behind.

"Whatever, whoever, man, woman—child even," muttered Emma.

Fiona was the first to volunteer. "I'll call the manager. I know her actually. I'm sure she'll be happy for us to collect money outside the supermarket for the parent education courses. Katy is artsy. We could ask her to work on the posters."

Alison responded, "You're right, but Katy's not here to be asked."

Fiona retorted, "What's being a volunteer all about? Don't you get nudged into things all the time? Isn't that part of the package deal when you're a volunteer?"

Alison countered, "Actually, I started coming to the coffee group to meet people. They gave me five weeks, and then they said, 'Oh, why don't you come along to the meetings to help us organize the next catering event? We have great fun, and we have wine and nibbles.'"

Emma intervened. "I'll bring wine and better nibbles next meeting. Sorry, Alison." Everyone laughed and the tension dropped a little. Alison looked down at her notes, thinking of her three friends who had joined the committee with her. They recently decided they didn't have time for Parents First anymore, since they started helping with classroom-based reading programs when their older children began school. Alison felt their absence keenly, especially since the remaining committee members didn't always seem to respond favorably to her suggestions for innovation and her determination to push programs forward. Alison worked in a government-funded child mental health policy team and could see the importance of developing parents' skills.

Margie called the meeting back to order. "Hey, we haven't talked about who will call around to drum up people to do the shifts outside the supermarket."

Noreen shifted uncomfortably in her seat. "I hate cold-calling like that. I really do."

Alison pondered out loud, "Emma does all the minutes and agenda. Margie does the accounts …"

Emma interrupted again at this juncture. "There's no sense in pointing fingers, Alison. People should only do what they're comfortable doing. I'm going to make some coffee. Come and help me, Margie."

The remaining three sat very still, until Fiona broke the silence. "Okay, so who's going to do it?"

Noreen frowned. "Well, I don't like making the calls, but I'll make the list of people to call." Alison sighed and agreed to make phone contacts from work. She was annoyed because she felt that the others used her paid work position as an excuse to give her all the jobs nobody else wanted. More than that, at the next meeting, the others would probably accuse her of trying to run the show again because it would fall to her to report on the number of collectors on the day.

Post-Meeting Conversations

After Margie, Alison, and Noreen left, Emma stacked the chairs and turned off the lights. She frowned and commented to Fiona, "I don't know why Alison gets so uptight about contributing to the committee and is so reluctant about taking on jobs. I mean, what does she want? More recognition? *I* don't expect a pat on the back for everything I do when I volunteer. You've got to feel goodness about it in yourself, that feeling of 'Wow I did that!' That's the buzz of it."

Fiona reflected, "I guess that for some people, it's a 'Get out of Jail Free' card. You know, if you volunteer, then you must be a good person, so you do it to show other people that you're nicer than you really are. Are you going to talk to Alison about her attitude?"

As they left the building, Emma commented, "I'm not sure. I mean, who am I to tell her what to do? We're all volunteers, so how can I tell her she's not really performing as expected?"

Alison sat in the front seat of her car, watching Fiona talking to Emma as they locked the clinic. Parents First had been framed from the outset as a "women's society appealing to women," and gossip was impossible to avoid in an organization where all the volunteers were female. She found her cell phone under the list of collectors to call. She felt relieved when her best friend picked up her phone immediately. Alison's frustration spilled out as she spoke: "I've had it up to here with the way the committee is running, of being excluded from the way the decisions are made. I want to leave, but I don't want to let them think they've got the better of me."

The Return Home

Margie walked across the parking lot, smiling. The planning for the new coffee groups had put all the meal preparation, diapers, and shopping lists back into perspective. Yet arriving home was even more difficult than leaving it had been. David sat tensely on the couch: "You know that I don't like you to go out so much during the week. I would rather you were home with me. I work all day to make it possible for you to spend time with us." Margie knew he was upset and wondered if she could continue to balance it all.

KEY TERMS

> **Conflict** - patterns of interaction between interdependent individuals, who perceive that others have incompatible goals or values.
>
> **Dialectical Tensions** - contradictions or opposing forces that are present within interpersonal or organizational relationships.
>
> **Organizational Commitment** - continued organizational membership, due to shared values, emotional attachment, benefits received, or obligation.
>
> **Voluntary Organizational Exit** - the process of leaving an organization, due to disenchantment with organizational mission or practices, or life circumstances that are incompatible with organizational engagement.

DISCUSSION QUESTIONS

1. Much of the literature frames volunteering as a free, individual decision. How do relationships, developed through volunteering, extend or challenge this view?
2. What issues does the case raise about volunteer work/family balance? What strategies could Parents First implement to help volunteers manage their commitments?
3. Many volunteers want organizations to acknowledge the role that family members play in enabling volunteering. How could *Parents First* improve volunteer retention through family-friendliness?
4. In what ways did conflict at home, related to volunteering, impact committee relationships?
5. Interpersonal relationships contain a number of dialectical tensions (connection/autonomy; certainty/uncertainty; openness/closeness). How does the data suggest that volunteers managed their need for connection within the committee and their desire for autonomy? What other dialectical tensions might also apply?
6. Volunteers frequently comment on the difficulty of "directing" other volunteers, due to the assumption that volunteer relationships should be participatory and collaborative. How were the patterns of organizing within the committee similar or different to the ways in which the women organized their husbands, partners, and children?
7. How might the communication patterns and decision-making styles change if the committee were entirely male or contained both men and women?

SUGGESTED READINGS

Farmer, S. M., & Fedor, D. B. (1999). Volunteer participation and withdrawal: A psychological contract perspective on the role of expectations and organizational support. *Nonprofit Management & Leadership, 9*, 349–367. doi: 10.1002/nml.9402

Haski-Leventhal, D., & Cnaan, R. (2009). Group processes and volunteering: Using groups to enhance volunteerism. *Administration in Social Work, 33*, 61–80. doi: 10.1080/03643100802508635

Marshall, G. A., & Taniguchi, H. (2012). Good jobs, good deeds: The gender-specific influences of job characteristics on volunteering. *Voluntas, 23*, 213–235. doi: 10.1007/s11266-011-9188-2

McAllum, K. (2014). Meanings of organizational volunteering: Diverse volunteer pathways. *Management Communication Quarterly, 28*, 84–110. doi: 10.1177/0893318913517237

McNamee, L. G., & Peterson, B. L. (2014). Reconciling "third space/place": Toward a complementary dialectical understanding of volunteer management. *Management Communication Quarterly, 28*, 214–243. 1–30. doi: 10.1177/0893318914525472

KEYWORDS

volunteer relationships, organizational exit, volunteer work/family balance, dialectical tension

*This case study is based on dissertation research that examined the meanings that members of three NPOs in New Zealand gave to their volunteering, the impact of professionalization, and the patterns of collaboration and conflict that characterized organizational relationships. The case integrates observations from field notes and data from interviews with 15 volunteers from one of these organizations.

International Volunteering: Training, Acculturation, AND Identity

CHAPTER NINETEEN

Cross-Cultural Engagement AND THE Effectiveness OF Overseas NPOs

Peace Corps Volunteers in Gambia*

KIM FLETCHER AND MAY HONGMEI GAO

Kennesaw State University

Part I: Training

Colleen and David landed in Gambia, a small English-speaking country in West Africa, with a group of 23 volunteers. Colleen was accepted to the Peace Corps for her background in web design, and so she was surprised to learn of her assignment in the Corps' education sector. David already taught science in the US, and he was excited to begin his service.

Prior to leaving, the volunteers spent three days in Washington, DC, for a crash course in culture shock and adjustment to life overseas. They learned that they should expect a "honeymoon" phase during which everything would appear new, different, and exciting, followed by a dis-integration or isolation period when they might be homesick, overwhelmed, or hostile toward the new culture. Finally, they would possibly experience a last stage of fitting in and happiness, if they chose to get to know the local people and adapt to local customs.

Colleen was still mulling over a quote she found in the volunteer handbook, which stated: "Being in the Peace Corps is like wearing a bunny suit while standing on a crowded street corner in New York, walking up to someone, and saying in a funny accent, 'Hi, I'm here to help!'" Six months ago, when assigned to Gambia, she had to look it up on a map. Before then she didn't even know the country existed. Looking at the task ahead, she wondered what she could possibly bring to the table with her limited understanding of the country's people, culture, history, or needs.

The next three months after arriving in Gambia were designed to bridge that knowledge gap. All Peace Corps volunteers go through a 12-week training period during which they spend time in a local village, learn the local language, and gain a better understanding of the culture. Several villages were used as training sites, with each village hosting three to four volunteers. The volunteers spent their days in language and cultural training classes, while spending nights with host families for intercultural immersion.

On the first day, David learned to say, "Hello, peace be unto you," "You also," "My name is David," and "Thank you." That night, one of the several wives in his host family brought out dinner, so he said, "Thank you," and he crouched on the ground to share the food bowl. A few bites in, David looked up and realized he was surrounded by women. The men were about 10 yards away, encircling another bowl. Embarrassed, David stood up, pointed to the men and himself, said, "Thank you" again, and walked over to the men's bowl. The next morning, David told his story to Modou, their trainer. "Don't worry." Modou laughed. "You'll do something worse by the time you leave."

Over the next several weeks, David, Colleen, and the other volunteers learned about the many social, historical, and cultural differences between Gambia and the US. Modou taught them that while English was the official language used in schools and public offices, less than 5% of Gambians spoke it. The majority spoke one or more of the several local languages that divide the country into linguistic and sometimes cultural enclaves. Modou also discussed the gender hierarchy, collectivist orientation, and more fluid notion of time present in Gambia. David and Colleen understood the concepts, but they did not fully grasp the effects the differences would have on their work until they arrived at their assigned sites.

In the last week of the training, David, Colleen, and the others were brought back to the Gambian capital to take a local language test. After they passed, they were given their final site assignments. Colleen was sent to a high school just across the river from the capital, while David was assigned to an elementary school with 100 students in a more remote area.

The day before leaving for their sites, the group met with the country director, who oversaw the 120 volunteers serving Gambia. She tried to give them a realistic expectation of what they would accomplish. "You might be expecting to do this much," she said, spreading her arms wide. "And maybe you'll do this much," she continued, bringing her hands a few centimeters apart, "but you'll have done something, and you'll have a better understanding of the world around you, and that's what counts." The director reminded them to stay in contact with their sector supervisors about their projects and their whereabouts and ended by thanking them for their service and wishing them luck. Colleen appreciated the candid and practical speech, but David felt less than inspired as he climbed in the car to go to his site.

Part II: At Volunteer Sites

One of the things Colleen loved about the Peace Corps was that the organization did not dictate projects. Local schools, businesses, or villages applied for volunteers based on perceived needs, and the Peace Corps matched the skills of the volunteers with the needs of the communities. In theory, this "matching" implied that when volunteers reached their sites, they would have a job and a project that fit their skill set. In practice, such matching did not always work as planned. Host communities did not always truly know their needs before the volunteers arrived, a volunteer may have terminated service during the training period, leaving a gap to be filled, or the needs of the communities may have changed before the volunteers arrived.

In Colleen's case, she was assigned to teach introductory computing at a high school. However, two weeks into her service, the school's science teacher left the country. The students came to her and asked if she was willing to teach the science courses, because "she's American," which somehow qualified her. Colleen had not taken a chemistry or biology course since her freshman year in college, but after flipping through the textbook, she thought she could handle it, and so she agreed. That week, she laid out her curriculum, cleaned the classroom, and then started teaching both the computing and science courses the next Monday.

The limited resources and Colleen's American-accented English led to some minor obstacles in the classroom, but she found ways to keep her students engaged and work around the language barrier. There were other problems, though, that troubled her more. First, she found that her students often "helped" one another on exams. When she confronted them about it, they seemed trapped. On one hand, the students knew that cheating was wrong. They called it "giraffing" (for the long neck it took to look over someone else's paper) and publicly pointed out the giraffes during tests. On the other hand, in collectivistic Gambia, those who were cheated off of felt they would be branded "wicked" if they did not help. Cheating off another student was against school rules, but not helping someone in need was also frowned upon.

Colleen also had some problems with her host family. They were open, caring, and treated her very well, but she felt that as a female teacher, she was a source of tension in the home. Though schooling in Gambia was mandatory, the law was not strictly enforced, and her seven-year-old host sister was not in school. When Colleen asked the father why, he said that schooling would get in the way of her work, and no one would marry her if she were too educated. He argued that it was a waste of time to educate a girl who would drop out when she was old enough to have children.

Farther up-country, David was having his own struggles. Classes did not start until three weeks into the semester. The first week was dedicated to registration of the students, which was done by hand in a spiral-bound notebook. The principal also registered students for bicycles that a Denmark-based NGO donated to the school. The bicycles were supposed to provide a means of transportation for students who lived more than 2 miles from school. The principal was to collect a fee for their use to pay for any needed repairs, but he felt that charging the fee would make the bikes inaccessible to most students, so he chose to provide them for free. During the second week, the students cleaned the classrooms and schoolyard, while the teachers and administrators discussed course assignments and classroom schedules. David was assigned to fifth and sixth grade science, seventh and eighth grade math, and bicycle maintenance.

Once David's classes started, they went well in the classroom. He really enjoyed teaching math in a new way to students who were used to rote-memory learning. His interactive, Socratic style engaged them in the material, and he felt they were making progress.

The bicycle maintenance was another story. While the bikes were given to individual students, entire villages were using them. In Gambia, if a child was given a bike, it became the shared property of her family and friends. Between overuse and harsh road conditions, the bikes quickly fell apart. Hole-filled tubes, broken axles, and rusted chains littered David's office. He could sometimes fix the bikes, but they often required new parts that simply were not available. Because there were soon not enough working bicycles for every student who needed one, the principal decided the best course of action would be to collect all the bikes so no one could use them. David tried to protest, arguing that those who took care of their bikes should be able to keep them, but in the end the principal's decision stood.

For David, the external struggles at work were a nuisance, but they were relatively easy to deal with. Where he was most uncomfortable was an internal feeling that he was losing his identity. In the US, David's friends considered him laid-back, kind, fun-loving, and quick-witted. In Gambia, though, he felt that his colleagues and host family had a different impression. His wordplay was met with blank stares, and his teasing of fellow teachers was viewed as rude. He wanted to be seen as "himself," but he was starting to realize that in order to be seen the same, he would have to act differently. To be considered "witty," he would have to learn a new brand of humor. To be considered "kind," he would have to give away much of his personal property. Both of these changes seemed to contradict major goals of the Peace Corps, which included promoting a better understanding of Americans on the part of those overseas, and doing so while engaging in sustainable efforts. He felt trapped, as he wanted to be perceived the same way he was in the US while working toward his organization's greater goals in Gambia.

KEY TERMS

Acculturation - the process of learning a new culture.

Ascription - the impression of a person in the mind of others in the community.

Avowal - an image one wants to project of him/herself to the community.

Collectivism - the character of a society in which the interest of the group is more important than that of the individual.

Culture Shock - a temporary feeling of dis-integration or disorientation that people often feel when they are exposed to an unfamiliar culture or set of values and behaviors.

Home Country - the country where one is born and raised.

Host Country - the foreign country where one migrates.

Time Concept - a culture's attitude toward time, which causes monochromic time people to be punctual and polychromic time people to be "relaxed" with time.

DISCUSSION QUESTIONS

Part I

1. The Peace Corps strives to prepare volunteers well before sending them overseas. What are some aspects of the training program that will help David and Colleen be more effective at their final sites? What can other organizations learn from the experience of the Peace Corps in doing volunteer work overseas?

2. Keeping in mind that project directives come from local communities rather than "above," what should be the role of the country director in managing and communicating with volunteers?

3. From a recruitment and retention perspective, should volunteers be given a realistic expectation of what they will accomplish, or should they be encouraged to "dream big"?

Part II

4. Some of the obstacles volunteers face stem from differences between the individualist American culture and collectivist cultures of most aid-receiving countries, such as Gambia.

   a. What are some of the obstacles illustrated in the story?

   b. At what point, or by whom, should these obstacles be addressed?

    c. Are there any general principles that can be applied to help US organizations be more effective in collectivist countries?

5. The volunteers face several obstacles due to the differences in orientation toward time.

    a. What are some of the obstacles illustrated in the story?

    b. What are some general principles that can be applied to help organizations guide their members regarding the time concept in different cultural contexts?

6. The Peace Corps has one of the best training programs for workers engaged in cross-cultural work, but roughly one-third of volunteers end their terms of service early because of many of the frustrations outlined in this story. What can NPOs do to reduce stress and burnout of employees, ease the acculturation process, and reduce attrition rates?

7. The story illustrates that the value orientations of the volunteers and those of the people they are working with do not always align.

    a. From an organizational perspective, what can or should be done when there is a mismatch between the values of the organization and of those it is trying to serve?

    b. What should be the volunteers' role or responsibility when their own cultural norms are different from the values or beliefs of those with whom they work?

8. Overseas workers often experience a similar problem to David's in that their identity avowal does not seem to match their identity ascription.

    a. In what ways might these identity issues affect American workers' abilities to express their ideas in an international context?

    b. Do organizations that work overseas have an obligation to help workers and volunteers address this problem? If so, how?

SUGGESTED READINGS

BBC News. (2014). The Gambia profile. Retrieved from http://www.bbc.com/news/world-africa-13376517

Gao, H. (2006). Overcoming obstacles: American expatriates striving to learn Chinese culture. *Global Business Languages, 11*, 31–53.

Gao, M. H., & Prime, P. (2010). Facilitators and obstacles of American companies in China: The UPS case. *Global Business Languages, 15*, 48–75.

Martin, J. N., & Nakayama, T. K. (2013). *Intercultural communication in contexts.* Boston, MA: McGraw-Hill.

National Archives. (n.d.). Founding documents of the Peace Corps: Background. Retrieved from http://www.archives.gov/education/lessons/peace-corps/

Neuliep, J. W. (2006). *Intercultural communication: A contextual approach* (3rd ed.). Thousand Oaks, CA: Sage.

KEYWORDS

intercultural communication, acculturation, overseas operations, Peace Corps

*This case is the amalgamation of experiences recorded in Gambian Peace Corps volunteers' blogs. Forty-six blogs from volunteers serving in the education sector from 2002 to 2009 were included in the analysis.

CHAPTER TWENTY

Learning BY Doing

Medical Volunteerism in India*

SANT KUMAR

San Francisco Veterans Administration Medical Center

CHRISTOPHER J. KOENIG

San Francisco Veterans Administration Medical Center &
University of California, San Francisco

The Shriram Health Clinic was located approximately an hour drive from New Delhi, India. The sights and smells of the slums where the clinic was located were foreign to Sunila, an American medical student volunteer whose parents emigrated from India when she was two years old. As Sunila and the other medical volunteers walked up to the clinic, a man led a group of donkeys through a pile of feces, which was likely from the cattle in the street next to the clinic. International Volunteer Headquarters sponsored the clinic every one to two weeks if there were enough volunteers to staff it. The clinic was held in an outdoor temple area in which local people held religious ceremonies and celebrated community events, such as birthdays or childbirths. Two local women, Namish and Chandi, and a local doctor, Dr. Prabodh, led the clinic, which was made up of four tables scattered throughout the courtyard. Each table had three volunteers who played a specialized role in the medical visit: (1) chief complaint; (2) vitals and patient history; (3) physical exam; (4) diagnosis and treatment. Each group sat at one station for the entire day with one chair reserved for a patient. Before patients entered, an elderly woman dressed in a blue sari lit incense in the temple and recited a prayer.

Local people lined up wearing ironed dress pants with collared shirts and bright saris with gold rings. This surprised Sunila, as she did not expect people living in the slum to wear such nice clothes to a doctor's visit. She mentioned this to Dr. Prabodh, who said, "For some patients, this is the first time ever seeing a doctor. For others, this may be the second or third time they have *ever* been to the doctor. So people wear their very best clothing." He paused, observing Sunila for a reaction, but she shrugged and moved to the chief complaint station to start work.

Ankur, a young man in his early 20s, limped through the clinic doors. He wore dark pants and a pressed, collared shirt. His hair was neatly combed to the right side. His teeth were yellow, and the upper row had grown over the bottom. His cheekbones stuck sharply out of his face. At the first station, Sunila asked to see his foot. Ankur did not understand English, and Sunila's Hindi was basic, so she asked Chandi to orally interpret the question. Ankur did not respond but slowly showed his foot, revealing a golf-ball-size swelling just above his heel. The entire foot was very discolored with shades of purple, red, and yellow. With Chandi interpreting, Sunila asked how he hurt his foot, and he replied, "I fell off a roof three days ago," and looked away to avoid eye contact with Sunila and Chandi. Sunila and the other volunteers at her station finished their notes and guided him to the next station.

Brett, a paramedic student from Australia, took Ankur's vitals and patient history—pulse, blood pressure, temperature, breaths per minute, and pupil dilation—all of which were normal. However, he noticed that Ankur had oddly low oxygen saturation, which could indicate a pulmonary problem. When Dr. Pradobh passed nearby, Brett called him over. Dr. Pradobh did not acknowledge Ankur but carefully examined the discolored foot. Noticing the patient's body odor, he covered his nostrils with his forefinger and soon retrieved a surgical mask and placed it over his mouth. Though Brett also noticed the body odor, he was surprised to see Dr. Prabodh's reaction. Without looking at Ankur, Dr. Prabodh asked Brett and the other volunteers in English the results of their investigations. Brett reported the chief complaint and vitals and told him that Ankur had a fracture. Dr. Prabodh nodded and said that Ankur must have an X-ray to determine the extent of the damage. "Most patients cannot afford an X-ray," he said, "but a charity hospital can give an X-ray for much less money than a public hospital." Brett also told him that Ankur had a low oxygen saturation count. Without telling Ankur what they discussed, Dr. Prabodh looked closely at his eyes and, again in English, commented that Ankur had eye degeneration and should be checked for tuberculosis. He did not repeat this in Hindi. Ankur, meanwhile, looked nervously at all the people around him but said nothing.

Dr. Prabodh glanced at the patients who continued to line up outside the clinic and unhurriedly turned back to Ankur. He told Ankur in Hindi that he needed an X-ray, but Ankur refused by shaking his head from side to side. Ankur curtly told Dr. Prabodh that he wanted pain medication. Dr. Prabodh repeated that Ankur should get an X-ray, and told him he should be checked for tuberculosis. After Ankur bobbed his head "no" again, Dr. Prabodh told him to proceed to the diagnosis and treatment station. Brett asked Dr. Prabodh what would happen next. Dr. Prabodh said that he will advise Ankur to go to the hospital, but he would also give him pain medication. He said that patients often take medications for a couple of days but often do not follow up. Brett asked why.

"There are many reasons. Sometimes, patients think that God will take care of them. Other times a relative might give another medication," Dr. Prabodh said, "but sometimes they do not like how they feel when they take the medicine, or they do not have enough money for more medication. Many patients do not even take the medication if they are given it. And even if they do take the medication, they may not get better because they need blood tests to solve the real problem, which most cannot afford." As Dr. Prabodh walked away, Sunila elicited the chief complaint in broken Hindi from the next patient who sat down at their station while Brett and another volunteer watched.

Two days later, Sunila walked into the clinic compound followed by local children pointing and laughing at her. She noticed Ankur among the many patients waiting to be seen, but he walked into the clinic with less of a limp. Today, Sunila and Brett were at the vitals and patient history station together. She and Brett tried to ask him questions regarding how he felt and what he would like, which was orally interpreted through Namish, one of the regular clinic workers. Ankur told them that he had been taking the pain medication, which had helped. Ankur continued by saying that his mother had been applying a home remedy, heated turmeric and mustard oil spread over uncooked *roti*, a traditional Indian flat bread similar to pita bread, which was applied to his foot like a bandage. Sunila eyed his swollen foot, perhaps noticing that the swelling had seemed to decrease in the past two days. Brett asked Ankur to move his foot. Ankur rotated it a little but grimaced in pain. Sunila called Dr. Prabodh to consult.

Dr. Prabodh seemed to recognize Ankur but did not greet him. He looked at the volunteers' notes. Even though they were at the vitals and patient history station, Dr. Prabodh asked in English what they thought this patient should do. Dr. Prabodh, the volunteers, and Namish all stood around Ankur, who sat patiently in the designated patient chair. In Hindi, Ankur asked Dr. Prabodh for more medication, but Dr. Prabodh ignored him. Brett said that Ankur should get an X-ray and rest. Dr. Prabodh agreed and, in Hindi, told Ankur that he should rest if he wants the pain to go away. Ankur said, "My old father shakes too much to work. I am the eldest, and my siblings look up to me to provide the family money and food. My sister has very poor vision in her right eye and will go blind in it if she does not get an operation soon, but the operation costs more than 20,000 Rupees (approximately $330 US). So I cannot rest." As Namish interpreted, the other volunteer stared blankly at the ground, and Brett grimaced as if he could not swallow. Sunila looked directly at Ankur.

Neither Dr. Prabodh nor Namish reacted visibly. Sunila commented that Ankur had very low oxygen saturation. Dr. Prabodh asked, "What do you think may be the cause of his low oxygen saturation?" Sunila volunteered, "He has a respiratory infection." Dr. Prabodh nodded his head and asked, "What questions should you ask to find out more about this low oxygen?" The volunteers remained silent. Dr. Prabodh then asked, "If he does not have enough oxygen, what do you think would happen to him?" Brett said that he would have trouble breathing. Sunila mentioned that Ankur could cough a lot. Dr. Prabodh nodded his head. While this interaction was going on in English, Dr. Prabodh neither addressed nor spoke to Ankur, who patiently sat in the patient chair. Finally, Dr. Prabodh asked in Hindi, "Have you had tuberculosis?" Ankur said that he had it 12 months ago, but he took medication for nine months, and it went away. Dr. Prabodh asked if he had had a fever recently. Ankur said that he had been having fevers at night and coughing a lot for the past week and a half. Without replying, Dr. Prabodh calmly turned to Sunila and Brett and said that tuberculosis had most likely returned. Silence resonated in the air as if the temple gong had been struck.

Sunila commented, "Wow. We went from a foot fracture to tuberculosis in less than five minutes. And we all touched him. Just kidding. I shouldn't think like that."

Brett replied, "It's okay. You're human." The news quickly spread to volunteers at other stations, and they donned surgical masks over their mouths and noses, newly aware that patients who come to Shriram Clinic often have serious but invisible illnesses. Behind them, the elderly woman knelt on the temple floor and lit incense, just as she had on previous days.

In Hindi, Dr. Prabodh told Ankur that he may have tuberculosis again and should be tested. He gave Ankur the name of his charity hospital and said to go there tomorrow. Unlike the previous recommendation, Ankur readily agreed by nodding his head to the side once. Before Ankur left the clinic, Dr. Prabodh gave him more pain medication. Like Ankur's first visit, Dr. Prabodh did not explain the directions of taking the medications or possible side effects. He only handed Ankur the carton.

After Ankur left, Brett and Sunila talked about his visit while the other volunteers listened wide-eyed.

"The foot fracture is very common, obviously," Jim said, "but on all the ride-alongs and clinicals, I don't think I've seen a fracture turn to TB."

"I'm so much more used to acute problems," said Sunila.

"Yeah, it's weird," said Jim. "Everyone here seems to suffer from more than one thing, but it's all related. They'll complain of leg pain, but it's connected to a fever they have, and then the fever is connected to some infection or disease."

"It makes it so hard to diagnose a patient," said Sunila. "Like, I'm good at diagnosing, but here I can get the first level but not the main one. It's pretty impressive how Dr. Prabodh knows like right away what the patient has."

"Yeah, definitely," said Jim. "He seems to know what patients suffer from even before talking to them."

On the last day of the clinic, Sunila saw Ankur again as he stood with a group of friends. He was leaning on his left foot. His friend wore similar clothes—dress pants and a collared shirt. As Sunila passed him, she made eye contact. Ankur didn't seem to recognize her, but she smiled at the local children pointing and laughing at her. Throughout her last day at the clinic, Sunila thought about Ankur. What will happen to Ankur? How many 23-year-old patients had similar family, economic, and medical situations to Ankur? How would a US doctor treat Ankur? What kind of medical care would Ankur receive if he were to immigrate to the US? The last question resonated with all of the volunteers like a plucked guitar string: Could I have done anything more to help him get the care he needed?

KEY TERMS

Culture - a complex, dynamic web of meanings that draws on the values, perspectives, and especially the taken-for-granted practices co-constructed by individuals as they interact with structural processes and local contexts over time.

Participatory Action Research - a type of inquiry that uses reflection on experience to understand the relationship among practices, situations, and social relationships to enhance decision making and to increase capacity for change.

Social Identity - a person's collection of believes about herself or himself based upon real or perceived membership in a group.

Voice - the linguistic construction of personhood through which social identities are represented, performed, transformed, evaluated, and contested.

DISCUSSION QUESTIONS

Culture

1. What facets of Indian culture are evident from the narrative? What facets of medical culture are illustrated? What facets of volunteer culture are illustrated?
2. What aspects of medical culture might be shared internationally? What aspects of medical culture might be unique to India? What role do social and ecological contexts play in these differences and similarities?
3. How does Dr. Prabodh's prior experience shape his interaction with Ankur? How does the volunteers' prior experience shape their reactions to how Dr. Prabodh treats Ankur?

Social Identity and Voice

4. What are some ways Dr. Prabodh's communication practices exclude Ankur from participating in the clinic visit? How do Ankur's communication practices exclude him from full participation in medical care? What choices do Dr. Prabodh, Ankur, and the volunteers have in the situation to change opportunities for individuals' to have voice?

5. Volunteers typically have expectations about what *volunteerism* means before arriving at a site. How might these expectations shape volunteers' perceptions of their role before and after working at the clinic?

6. Sunila occupies a special position relative to the other volunteers—she is both Asian Indian and American. How do her cultural, interpersonal, and individual identities shift throughout the narrative? What advantages and disadvantages might there be to being a partial member of a group during a volunteer experience?

SUGGESTED READINGS

Dutta, M. J. (2007). Communicating about culture and health: Theorizing culture-centered and cultural sensitivity approaches. *Communication Theory*, 7, 304–328. doi: 10.1111/j.1468-2885.2007.00297.x

Koenig, C. J., Dutta, M. J., Kandula, N., & Palaniappan, L. (2012). "All of those things we don't eat": A culture-centered approach to dietary health meanings for Asian Indians living in the United States. *Health Communication*, 27, 818–828. doi: 10.1080/10410236.2011.651708

KEYWORDS

culture, voice, social identity, participatory action research, healthcare

*This case study is based on research conducted as part of an ongoing investigation into the global health experiences of premedical and medical students. The data were field notes composed of observations, informal and formal interviews, and the first author's personal reflections about his volunteer experience as a medical volunteer in Faridabad, India, in December of 2013 and January of 2014.

Fundraising AS A Profession: Socialization AND Loyalty

CHAPTER TWENTY-ONE

The New Girl*

JESSICA MARTIN CARVER

Western Kentucky University

Kaitlynn Smith, a young professional, had recently read about the steady growth of higher education fundraising as an occupational field. So when Kaitlynn was offered the position of the new director of development for the College of Basic and Applied Sciences for High Top University (HTU), she jumped at the new opportunity to work as a major gifts officer. HTU was a private institution and housed the High Top University Foundation, a registered 501(c)(3), where all of the donations to the university were held. At HTU, a gift of $10,000 or more constituted a major gift, which made her both nervous and excited as she embarked on this journey.

Her first week went well, and she immediately got the feeling that she was going to get along well with her coworkers, supervisors, and the dean of the college. Most importantly, she thought she would thoroughly enjoy a position in higher education fundraising. She got the sense that this work was noble and necessary for the advancement of HTU as a whole, its programs, and students. Kaitlynn spent her first few days being introduced to individuals in the division and becoming familiar with their roles in the unit of Alumni and Development. She was trained on how to use HTU's database system, where she learned how to look up individual donors and alumni. She even viewed past contact reports, which gave information on previous visits or touch-points the person had with other development professionals or people at HTU. She also inherited a portfolio of alumni and donor names from her predecessor. This portfolio contained names of individuals who should be top on her list to visit and approach about making contributions to the college and HTU.

At the start of her second week, Kaitlynn was eager to attend her first major gift officer meeting. She was told to bring her new portfolio of names because the group would be reviewing "prospects" and donors at this gathering. This meeting consisted of all the directors of development from their respective colleges, as well as the assistant vice president for major gifts, Cheryl, who led the meeting. Cheryl started the meeting by welcoming Kaitlynn to the unit and giving encouraging words and expressing her belief in Kaitlynn's potential success. After the warm introduction, they got right to work as Cheryl asked, "Who wants to start this week's prospect and donor discussion?"

Jack, director of development for the College of Business, chimed in. "I'll go. I've been trying to get a visit with Don Groper, president of TopSales, and his receptionist is screening all of his calls and serving as his gatekeeper. I've tried sending e-mails but haven't got a response. Does anyone have any ideas?"

Cheryl retorted, "Groper's got great giving potential and ranks high on all our wealth screenings. This is definitely a top prospect that we want to get in with."

There was a brief lull in conversation before Sandra, director of development for the College of Health Sciences, whipped out some suggestions, "Does he have LinkedIn, and have you tried connecting with him? You could also check out his other connections and see if any of our current donors or board members could make an introduction or help us get more personal contact information."

Jack was pleased with this suggestion and responded, "I'll give that a shot! Groper is so prominent; surely we can get one of our close-knit alumni who already has a relationship with HTU to pin him down for a visit."

Cheryl continued. "Good idea. Sandra, now what or who are you working on?"

Sandra paused to decide which prospective donor she should bring up and then shared, "Well, I have a few different projects going on, but my dean would like to focus on naming opportunities for our new College of Health Sciences building. The Joneses are such loyal supporters and should be ready if I hit them up for another gift. I'm thinking they can name one of the labs."

Cheryl nodded. "You're right. They're prime for the picking, and this is a good project to bring them in on. How much are the labs because they have a lot of capacity?"

Sandra responded, "The labs are 100K. Their wealth capacity rating was determined to be around $250,000 to $500,000, so they should easily be able to do $100,000, especially if it is a multiyear pledge. We're still fishing for prospects. I had our research department pull a list of potential donors for the building. They started by getting names of individuals who've given to the College of Health Sciences, are looking at pulling names from the wealthiest zip codes in the surrounding areas and other graduates with nice titles such as VP and president. The list will also include LYBUNTs (gave Last Year But Unfortunately Not This year), SYBUNTs (gave Some Years But Unfortunately Not This year), never-givens, and other worthy suspects. Hopefully, we can eliminate those prospects with cobwebs in their wallets."

Cheryl looked satisfied and said, "Good work. Keep me updated on your progress with the Joneses, and we can work on getting a proposal in front of them. I'm glad that you're looking to take them up a level from their last scholarship endowment gift of $50,000. Also, make sure to send me that list from the research department, as President Martin may be able to help provide insight or even leverage some gifts and ask for higher amounts. Jordan, you're up."

Jordan, the director of development for the College of Education, piped up. "Well, I have a couple of those 'millionaire next door types' who may not be able to make a current gift but have the capacity to leave us a fortune in the form of a bequest."

Cheryl inquired, "Oh? Who are the prospects and what is the next step?"

Jordan replied, "Sally Johnson is single, never married, has no children, and responded to a mailing we sent out about planned giving. She marked the response device option that she was considering a gift in her estate to HTU. I've set up a visit with her and will thank her for her consideration and hopefully get an idea of how much capacity she has. The other individual, Dr. James Carpenter, again, has no children and never married. He's a retired faculty member who is considering a charitable gift annuity (CGA) and would like to pay back HTU for his successful career. I'll ask him if I can draw him up a scenario showing him the benefits of a CGA and see where he is in relation to actually making the gift."

"Very good, keep us updated on your visit with Ms. Johnson," Cheryl replied. She then looked to Kaitlynn and asked if she had any questions or had had a chance to prioritize her inherited portfolio.

Kaitlynn had excitedly done some research already. She was a bit uneasy about publicly discussing an individual's personal wealth in this way but calmly said, "I've read past contact reports for several individuals on my list. I'm trying to strategically think through who I need to go see in my first month, quarter, six months, etcetera. I also plan to take this list to the dean and discuss with him further to get his feedback." To Kaitlynn, breaking down the list in time-based goals seemed like a better option than personal wealth-based goals.

Cheryl accepted Kaitlynn's answer and applauded her ambition to get started so quickly. "Good start, but one suggestion would be to make sure research has given each donor a wealth score. This will help you to arrange your list effectively in order to get the best return on investment."

The meeting continued like this, with Cheryl bringing up other names and checking in on past HTU donors and their current status. Kaitlynn reluctantly participated but could not help but be bothered by the nonchalant way donors were referred to as metaphors or just one component of who they are, which happened to be their wealth, giving history, or ability to give.

When the meeting adjourned, Kaitlynn was anxious to discuss the meeting with one of her new coworkers. After one week of work, she had already started to view Sandra as a mentor and felt as if she could confide her uneasiness to her new colleague. She decided to stop by her office and see if she had a minute to talk. She approached the door, and although the door was open, she knocked to get Sandra's attention and quietly said, "Do you have a moment?"

"Sure, what's up?" Sandra responded casually.

"I wanted to talk with you about our major gift meeting. I was just wondering if all of the conversations are like that, referring to donors in dollar amounts, ratings, and how much they can give."

Sandra smiled and reassuringly said, "I know it can sound intimidating and unthoughtful, but we, like any other occupation, have to use certain terminology that we all understand and can categorize. There are really two parts to our profession—the art and the science. The meeting you were just in is the science, and that's the part we have to do in order to identify and achieve the art, which is the part where you get to connect an individual and the institution and watch it grow into a meaningful relationship that ultimately ends in a gift."

"But aren't there other terms we could use instead of never-givens, suspects, or prime for the picking? It feels strange to talk about someone's personal wealth capacity like that."

"Things like never-givens, prospects, suspects, LYBUNTs, and SYBUNTs have almost become industry standards. We have our jargon just like any other line of work. It's very similar to sales, even though I would argue our work is for a nobler cause. Phrases like 'low-hanging fruit' or 'prime for the picking' are also common, but you don't have to use them. In order for us to best help HTU, we must know how much a person is capable of giving, and in the end, a donor is going to do what they are comfortable with. When you reach that point, it's more of an easy conversation and not an assessment of capacity or wealth screening."

Kaitlynn started to soften. "That makes sense, but I think it'll take some time to get used to. I'll be more prepared for the next meeting. Do you have any more advice for a new development professional?"

Sandra quickly divulged, "I think one of the main things you need to realize as a new fundraiser is that we always have to be 'on.' You'll quickly begin to realize that you're always representing the institution, even when you're not physically at work. You'll see your donors and prospects at the grocery store or ball games, and they may approach you to discuss work or the university. With technology, we can easily be reached at all hours of the day, so you're never fully unplugged."

Kaitlynn pondered and said, "I think I can handle that."

Sandra reiterated, "The most important thing you can do is to find or somehow create a balance. Try to define the blurred line of work and home life. If you're going to answer work e-mails at home, set an appropriated amount of time in the evening so you aren't constantly checking your phone. If you run into a donor at the grocery, make sure to tell them that you'll follow up the next day, so you don't feel the pressure of getting back to them that night. Always remember that the functions and events we attend are fun, but we are there to represent HTU and be a resource to those guests in attendance."

Kaitlynn responded, "I think like any profession, it'll take some time to get used to the jargon, tensions, and constraints of this job. But I think the rewards of encouraging donors and potential donors to give back to the institution will greatly outweigh any negative language or pressures of always being 'on.' Thanks for the advice, and I appreciate your candidness."

Sandra nodded, smiled with encouragement, and said, "Anytime."

Kaitlynn walked back to her office and felt better about the major gift meeting and the expectations in next week's gathering. She was again excited and greatly anticipated reviewing her list and prioritizing it, now that she didn't see it as quite a negative concept.

KEY TERMS

Metaphor - a linguistic device used to compare objects, activities, or ideas that are usually unrelated in nature to imply or give deeper or new meaning.

Organizational Assimilation - the process or stages that occur as individuals enter and leave organizations: (1) anticipatory socialization, (2) organizational encounter, (3) metamorphosis, and (4) disengagement or exit.

Socialization - a learning process where an individual is integrated into a group or organization and adapts or adjusts to its norms, culture, or activities.

Work-Life Balance - explores the tensions individuals experience while trying to balance professional (work) and personal (health, family, leisure, etc.) aspects of their lives.

DISCUSSION QUESTIONS

Metaphors in Nonprofit Fundraising

1. What metaphorical concepts are used in the major gift meeting? How might their language shape the ways in which they think about and approach potential donors?

2. How might the metaphors used negatively impact how others perceive the fundraising profession?
3. How might the metaphors used negatively impact how nonprofit fundraising professionals perceive their profession? Or their potential donors?

Work-Life Balance Issues in Nonprofit Fundraising

4. What kind of work-life balance concerns or situations could happen in nonprofit fundraising?
5. What are some ways a nonprofit fundraising professional might handle work-life balance issues?

Organizational Assimilation Theory in Nonprofit Fundraising

6. What stages of Organizational Assimilation Theory has Kaitlynn experienced in this case study?
7. What could Kaitlynn have done in the anticipatory assimilation phase to have better prepared her for a fundraising job?
8. What role is Sandra playing in the assimilation process?
9. What can nonprofit organizations do to socialize newcomers to the fundraising profession?

SUGGESTED READINGS

Greenhaus, J. H., & Beutell, N. J. (1985). Sources of conflict between work and family roles. *Academy of Management Review, 10*, 76–88. doi: 10.5465/AMR.1985.4277352

Kramer, M. W. (2010). Occupational and role anticipatory socialization. In *Organizational socialization: Joining and leaving organizations* (pp. 25–44). Malden, MA: Polity Press.

Turner, R. C. (1991). Metaphors fund raisers live by: Language and reality in fund raising. In D. F. Burlingame & L. J. Hulse (Eds.), *Taking fund raising seriously: Advancing the profession and practice of raising money* (pp. 37–50). San Francisco, CA: Jossey-Bass.

KEYWORDS

metaphor, socialization, work-life balance, fundraising, development

*This case study is based on two similar research projects conducted with 18 higher education development professionals. The specific data for this situation come from the 18 interviews of higher education fundraisers from both studies, as well as the author's experience as a higher education fundraiser. This particular case study does not reflect the view of all 18 participants but uses similar language and the perceptions from common language that were found.

CHAPTER TWENTY-TWO

Working Hard FOR Less Money?

Fundraisers, Loyalty, and Employee Retention*

REBECCA J. MEISENBACH AND JESSICA M. RICK

University of Missouri

Hi, Suzie, I'm Mark Jorgenson from Executive Search Consultants, Incorporated. Shay University has an opening in its development office for a major gifts officer. I would like to talk to you about whether you or anyone you know would be interested in this position. Please call me at 555–9842.

Suzie Franks, a major gifts development officer at her alma mater, Hairston University, listened to this voice mail in her office on Monday morning. Hairston was a moderately selective, nonprofit, private, liberal arts college in a midsize city in the eastern United States. Suzie loved Hairston, cheered proudly for its athletic teams, was grateful for her education there, and worked hard to help her school raise the large donations from wealthy individuals that were necessary to cover the gaps between the school's expenses and its tuition income. Mark was a headhunter for a more prestigious rival college in the same state. Suzie initially freaked out about the call and asked both her closest work friend, Nila, and her mentor, John, to go out to coffee that afternoon to talk about the message.

Suzie:	Do people here think I'm trying to leave? I can't believe he'd call and leave a message like that on my work phone.
John:	Oh, I know. I get those calls sometimes. I never return them.
Nila:	Why not?
John:	Because I feel like, almost, if I return the call, it's disloyal to Hairston.
Suzie:	Yes! I feel guilty they've even called me. What would our director think if she knew?

Nila: Oh, come on, guys. This man, Mark, is just trying to network. Suzie, it's okay to call him. You'll make a contact in the field. You have every right to hear him out.

John: Don't you dare leave us. I can't imagine you working for our rival.

Suzie: I know. I hate the Shay Bulldogs. Can you see me wearing their colors?

Suzie called Mark back on Tuesday and was surprised to learn that her experiences and skills were almost exactly what Shay University needed. "It'd be a nice promotion," she thought. The position also offered $20,000 more per year with better benefits. Suddenly, this "networking" conversation was a serious job possibility. Two weeks later, Suzie was offered the job at Shay University.

As a well-respected major gifts officer, Suzie helped Hairston University receive millions of donation dollars. She had worked at Hairston for five years, loved helping her alma mater, and wholeheartedly supported its mission of making a high-quality education available to a variety of students. She herself benefited from the university's need-blind admissions policy in which students were admitted to the school regardless of their financial ability and were guaranteed a loan and scholarship package that made attending possible. Shay University focused more on educating wealthy Americans, the majority of whom paid full tuition. Suzie had cheered against Shay for a decade and never thought she'd work for Hairston's rival. But the extra income would help her buy a house, and the position came with new opportunities for career advancement. Unsure of what to do, she sought advice from her coworkers since they had both faced similar situations.

Nila had worked in fundraising for nonprofit healthcare and educational organizations for over 13 years and at Hairston for two. Every three years or so, she took a new job, quickly earning promotions and raises because fundraisers can get better raises by moving externally than by staying within the same organization.

John, on the other hand, had stayed at Hairston University for his entire 17-year career, despite other offers. He formed strong, successful relationships with donors and was well respected across campus. Even though he had spent five more years in the field, his salary was under Nila's.

Suzie, Nila, and John went out for lunch to talk. Suzie shared that she was happy at Hairston but admitted that the extra income and career advancement would be helpful. When she asked for their advice, the conversation got somewhat heated.

Nila: Go for it! There is a reason I keep changing organizations. When I start a job, I have a year to get my feet wet. In the second year, they expect me to perform at a certain level, but if I do not meet their expectations, the organization believes things will get better the third year. And after the third year, I leave and move on to a new organization, where I make more money.

John:	Fundraising doesn't work well that way. You need to form personal connections with donors to see long-term results. I value the people I've met in this job. Many are my friends now. Donations extend from those relationships.
Nila:	You like befriending donors and forming personal relationships. But I disagree with you about what works; I'm working in fundraising to help the organization as a whole succeed and improve its fundraising practices.
John:	But you work with donors, too. You move on quickly and don't see the damage your departure does to the university!
Nila:	I don't damage the organizations I work for! I facilitate relationships between donors and the university. I'm the conduit for that. Anyone can be that conduit after I leave. I like working where I know I can have an impact. Suzie can go in, help them, and then move on.
John:	You mean she can share what has worked for us with a rival school? And how do you make any money for the organization that quickly? A large portion of my time is spent making connections for possible future donations. Successful fundraisers have been at their institution for a long period of time.
Nila:	That is only part of it. Fundraising needs people like you. But I like to go into organizations, implement what I learned from my previous experiences, and make a big splash. Then after a few years, I don't have any new tricks in my bag for this organization. I've implemented them all. And I've impressed everybody I'm going to impress. It's only downhill from there. I might as well get out while I'm on top.
John:	Yes, that may be true, and you know I love having you here. But that attitude isn't really part of what we do here. It costs money to replace you, maybe as much as we gain from your improvements to our process. The key to a good development office is the team in place. Right now, we have a good team. We bounce ideas off each other. We are involved in other coworkers' accounts. Why mess up a good thing? We're doing great things together for a cause I believe in.
Nila:	You just said that we are all helping each other. You know about Suzie's donors. You could help cover that transition if she leaves. The team can help out, and Suzie needs to make the best decision for her.
John:	But what's best for her is not that simple. Suzie has made those connections; I can't swoop in and take over those accounts. The donors will be confused and hurt. We'll lose some of your donors, Suzie. When Greg left, it took us months to get caught up, and two of the biggest donors he was working with aren't returning our calls. We can't magically replace the relationship Greg had with those people. We're working together to help this university and its students, just like other fundraisers worked hard to help you when you were a student, Suzie. When you leave, you hurt the university, and I know that will hurt you. How can you be thinking of leaving us for our biggest in-state rival?

Nila: How can you say no to that big of a promotion? Suzie should seriously consider this option. It's a great promotion and will be great for her career. She's been successful here; she can do it other places, too.

John: But part of her success here is the fact that we've worked so well together. Shay is struggling right now. They don't have that kind of chemistry in their office, and they don't have people who stay long. It's going to be a tougher job that requires longer hours and is much more stressful.

Nila: It's great that you've worked together for that long, but turnover in nonprofits is high; most fundraisers only stay at one organization for two to three years. We're in high demand. If she doesn't leave, someone else will.

John: I get that, but how can you go from working toward a meaningful cause like ours to working for "the man"?

Nila: She's not talking about working for a for-profit corporation. She's considering using her skills for another nonprofit. Why shouldn't we be paid well? Just because we're working in the nonprofit sector doesn't mean we need to be poor. We have valuable skills and should be paid well for them.

John: We are paid well enough, and I don't want to be paid more to help a cause I don't believe in. I'm proud to be part of this family because working for "education for everyone" is important to me. If I get paid more, that's money that can't go to educating a student.

Suzie: I guess I see your point. We ARE working in the nonprofit sector; we aren't supposed to be paid lots of money.

John: Working for a cause and the betterment of this university and its students is the reason that I do what I do—not the salary I make.

Nila: Why can't we do both? Just because Suzie might take a job that pays better doesn't mean she's not doing good things. It's a different mission and cause, but it's still important. You can work for a good cause and make really good money.

John: Many don't share that opinion. Newspapers are always making a fuss, printing negative stories on "high" nonprofit sector salaries. People get upset if we're making as much money as workers in the for-profit sector.

Suzie: So, actually, if I'm considering leaving the school that I really love, shouldn't I be considering for-profit work where I'd make even more money and no one would question me about it? My banking and administration skills would make me eligible for positions that easily pay $30,000 more than I make here.

John: Whoa. I wish we'd never encouraged you to answer Mark's message.

Suzie: I know, right? But I admit there are moments when I miss corporate America. When I worked at the bank, everyone respected and understood what I did for a living. I had more reasonable hours and my grandmother didn't call me a "glorified beggar."

Nila:	Nice.
Suzie:	You know how it is. That's what she thinks my job is. And my friends don't really get what we do in development. When I do explain, they always say things like, "Wow, I could never ask people for money." It gets tiring sometimes.
Nila:	I just tell people that it's my career, and I'm really happy to have a great job that pays my bills. It doesn't bother me.
John:	I've been called lots of things: tin cup beggar, beggar in a three-piece suit. I laugh it off. And when someone asks how I can ask people for money, I just say, "I'm not asking for me; I'm asking someone to support a worthy cause that I believe in and am proud to serve." Suzie, you need to think about that before you decide. How are you going to be successful at a school whose financial mission is so different from ours? Can you support and believe in the cause at Shay University?

Suzie listened carefully. Both friends made good points, and she had a lot to consider. After a few days of deliberation, Suzie called Mark to give him her decision.

Hi, Mark. This is Suzie. I have made a decision regarding your offer ...

KEY TERMS

Employee Retention - an organization's ability to keep employees working for that organization rather than leaving to work at another organization.

Identity - a self-concept that is constructed through personal and social interpretations of material realities and societal discourses.

Metaphors - a figure of speech in which the word for one thing is used to represent another thing.

Professional Fundraisers - organizational employees who raise money for a nonprofit organization.

Stigma - a discrediting identity mark typically associated with questionable physical, moral, and/or social status.

DISCUSSION QUESTIONS

Organizational Metaphors and Employee Retention

1. What distinct metaphors do you see John and Nila using to make sense of what they do as fundraisers for an NPO?

2. How does each of those metaphors justify their different attitudes toward switching jobs as a fundraiser?
3. What metaphors would you want to promote among fundraisers if you were in charge of retaining fundraising employees at Hairston University or another NPO?

Identity, Identification, and Stigma Management

4. Suzie shared that her grandmother has called her a "glorified beggar." If we understand this label as a stigmatizing message, how can fundraisers manage this negative identity?
5. How important do you think identifying with an organization and/or its mission is in being a good fundraiser? In working in the nonprofit sector in general?
6. What identity management issues do you think Suzie will face if she leaves Hairston University for either Shay University or a for-profit organization?

Making Money and Critical Theory

7. What are the arguments being offered for and against making a lot of money in nonprofit/public sector work?
8. What societal discourses (e.g., capitalism) do these arguments draw and build upon?
9. Whose/what interests do each of these arguments and discourses serve?

Overall

10. What would you do if you were Suzie?
11. What would you do if you were Suzie's boss at Hairston?

SUGGESTED READINGS

Brown, W. A., & Yoshioko, C. F. (2003). Mission attachment and satisfaction as factors in employee retention. *Nonprofit Management & Leadership, 14*, 5–18. doi: 10.1002/nml.18

Meisenbach, R. J. (2010). Stigma management communication: A theory and agenda for applied research on how individuals manage moments of stigmatized identity. *Journal of Applied Communication Research, 38*, 268–292. doi: 10.1080/00909882.2010.490841

Meisenbach, R. J. (2008). Working with tensions: Materiality, discourse, and (dis)empowerment in occupational identity negotiations among higher education fund raisers. *Management Communication Quarterly, 22*, 258–287. doi: 10.1177/0893318908323150

Smith, R. C., & Eisenberg, E. M. (1987). Conflict at Disneyland: A root-metaphor analysis. *Communication Monographs, 54*, 367–380. doi: 10.1080/03637758709390239

KEYWORDS

fundraisers, nonprofit employee retention, metaphors, stigma, identity management

*This case study was based on research focusing on identity and stigma management among higher education fundraisers. The first author has published work based on these data in *JACR*, *MCQ*, and a forthcoming book chapter. Many parts of the dialogue in this discussion among Nila, Suzie, and John are quotes from interviews with current and former fundraisers at higher education institutions in the United States.

Corporate Partners: Employee Giving AND Volunteering AT Work

CHAPTER TWENTY-THREE

Employee Volunteerism Programs AND Community Engagement

Commitment, Identification, and Impact*

ALYSSON M. SATTERLUND
Dartmouth College

STEVEN K. MAY
University of North Carolina at Chapel Hill

Monica lived through four bank mergers. Through each, she'd managed to get rehired and exceed her sales goals. But when Bob, a former boss, called and asked if she wanted to join him at the new Community State Bank (CSB), she resigned her position at Big Corporate Bank. By the day's end, she was the new customer service manager at CSB. Bob was ecstatic. CSB just opened its third branch and was expecting further growth. Deposits were up, not because his team secured a few large accounts but because they secured hundreds of smaller local accounts. He knew why: customers wanted to know the people with whom they entrusted their money. Over the last few years, this option had been difficult to find. Smaller banks had been increasingly "scooped up" by larger corporate banks through mergers and acquisitions, creating uncertainty and stress for employees and anonymity for customers who were accustomed to their having tellers greet them by name.

Bob's pride in challenging the "big boys" was evident in how he recruited customers and team members. For Bob, and the rest of the executive team, connecting to the community as members of the community was more than just a successful business strategy—it was a way of being. He lived this identity wholeheartedly and invited, cajoled, and encouraged others on his team to do the same. Monica finally felt that she was back where she belonged. She enjoyed spending her work-day among friends and with customers she cared about. She knew the names of her customers' children, and a few of them brought in her favorite candy on her birthday. CSB's success grew out of these experiences. But then September 11 happened. When the World Trade Center towers went down, Bob and his team were hundreds of miles away. Like many across the country, employees and cus-tomers at CSB collected money for the American Red Cross. Everyone felt that it was the least they could do, and, though small, it was important and felt good to do something. Soon after, the Employee Volunteer Program (EVP) was born with the encouragement of Bob and the support of many CSB employees.

To get the EVP off the ground, Monica volunteered to pull service opportuni-ties together for the upcoming holidays. She remembered meeting Lee, the direc-tor of Little City's food bank at a United Way event. Monica gave Lee a call and got his thoughts on how CSB could help. Monica had plenty of other job respon-sibilities, but like Bob had shared with her more than once, community banking involved living and serving in the community. Isn't that what made her different? Made them different than Big Corporate Bank? Until September 11, serving pri-marily involved her contributions to her son's school. Now she was responsible for creating volunteer opportunities for employees across the three branches. It seemed easy enough, and everyone was enthusiastic about it.

As the bank's customer service manager—and now the director of the com-pany's EVP—Monica began to read as much as possible regarding volunteerism trends. By reading professional publications about the nonprofit sector, she learned a number of interesting statistics. She discovered that, in 1985, 82 million people volunteered, and, despite a reduction in available leisure hours per week, 93 million Americans had volunteered in 1995. In 2001, 44% of adults volunteered time to a not-for-profit organization, and 5% of these adults were involved in work-related volunteer programs. So, she knew that her efforts at CSB were not unique and were part of a much larger trend toward volunteerism. From a more recent study, Monica learned that, in 2012, 64.5 million adults volunteered time to a not-for-profit orga-nization, and 1.4% of these adults were asked by their supervisor to volunteer.

After conducting this research, Monica asked Bob if she could learn more by attending a two-day conference on community engagement at a nearby university. The organizers were looking for business participants, and Monica thought that it would be an ideal place to learn more. Bob readily agreed and also asked Jim, the HR director, to attend. There were several key themes at the conference, with a focus on aligning the business goals of the company with community needs. For example, one prominent speaker, a local media company CEO, argued that cor-porate volunteerism was an important means to strengthen company brand and reputation. Using his own company as an example, he claimed that an EVP was an excellent way to convince both internal and external audiences of the organization's values. As he concluded his remarks, Monica took a quick glance at some of the conference's prepared materials. In them, she saw this quote from the CEO: "A profit-seeking firm should not get involved in volunteer activities simply out of altruism. You want to see your volunteerism and charity attract and build a productive workforce and raise your community profile, not to get your charitable jollies, because that distracts from your fundamental task, which is to make money."

The CEO's perspective on EVPs seemed so different from the approach they had developed at CSB, but his comments did make her reflect on the motivations for EVPs. During a short break, she jotted some questions in her conference notebook: What is our motivation for the EVP? What are we trying to accomplish and why? How do we balance meeting the company's bottom line and helping the community? How do nonprofit organizations approach EVPs while maintaining their missions?

The Community State Bank Employee Volunteer Program

The neighborhood was filled with modest homes, windows framed behind decorative bars, and small lawns. Bob and Monica drove in separate vehicles, both among a long caravan from CSB. Bob parked his Cadillac across the street from the first address and Monica pulled up behind in her Volvo. They had spent the morning filling boxes with Thanksgiving meal essentials dropped off by employees and customers at each of the bank's branch offices throughout the week.

Bob grabbed a box from his car trunk and walked across the street to the address provided to CSB by the United Way of Little City. He knocked on the door; no one answered. Bob knocked again but this time a little louder. After the second knock, an older African American woman answered the door. She looked at Bob, a well-groomed white man and stranger. She did not say a word. With the pride of a volunteer, however, Bob said, "When you enjoy this Thanksgiving meal, I hope you will think of Community State Bank." With silence, the woman accepted the box, stepped back in the house, and closed the door. Undaunted, Bob returned to his car to retrieve a second food box for another delivery. Jim, the HR director, took Bob's picture for the newsletter.

For the next few hours, this activity continued throughout the neighborhood. While delivering her first food box, Monica reflected on the satisfaction she felt from giving. She also felt gratitude and a sense of relief that her family was able to take for granted that they would not go without a warm meal at Thanksgiving. Monica remembered the conversation she'd had with Lee, at the food bank, when they discussed the volunteer project and the families that would receive the holiday food boxes. Lee had cautioned Monica that most families would be conflicted about receiving the food boxes. He reminded Monica that most of the parents worked full-time jobs and still had challenges making ends meet—especially during the holidays when extra money for gifts and special meals was not an option. Monica knew times were difficult all around; heating bills had skyrocketed this year and with almost all of the mills closed, folks without a college education had a difficult time getting out of poverty.

Back at work after the Thanksgiving deliveries, Jim seemed to be an even stronger advocate for the program than Monica had expected. "It's such a fantastic way to strengthen the sense of community—the culture—at the bank," he explained. "It is so satisfying to work together, as a team, to help other people."

"Do you think so?" Monica asked.

"Sure," Jim replied. "The EVP is a great way for employees to become more committed to Community State Bank." He went on to tell Monica about the various ways that organizational commitment would benefit the company. As HR director, he studied how organizational commitment was related to reduced absenteeism, reduced turnover, and employee innovativeness. "It has even been associated with increased job performance," Jim told her. Research, Jim explained, had also shown that employees who are committed to an organization believe their organization is a good place to work, don't look for other jobs, and believe that their current employer best fits their needs. They even require less supervision and work harder.

"It does seem like a win-win situation," Monica responded. "From what I can tell, we are making a difference in the community and people seem to really identify with the bank, as a result."

"Definitely," Jim agreed. "It's a great way to further motivate bank employees."

"It's true," Monica affirmed. "One of my concerns, though, is what we do with employees who don't feel strongly about participating in the EVP."

The members of CSB and those involved in supporting the EVP recognized that participation in the EVP allowed them to demonstrate their professional commitments to their workplace. Employee participants not only raised awareness of important community issues, but they also learned more about the experiences of others unlike themselves who also called Little City home. Employees who participated in the EVP reflected the type of community bank that Bob sought to build. Specifically, Bob and the rest of the leadership team recruited employees, like Monica, who would identify with a "community bank" that engaged in community service. Through the EVP, the bank's leaders wanted to inspire both organizational identification and commitment while also differentiating themselves from "corporate banks."

Several employees described how the integration between their own personal values and their commitment to, and identification with, the bank and its EVP motivated their participation. For example, Monica read an e-mail from Renee:

> *Giving to others who don't have nearly the blessings I have is important to me as a person of faith, just like it was important to my parents and the way I hope it will be important to my own children. I know I probably get more out of the EVP than those I help really get, and I have a lot of demands on my time, but this is really a way for me to connect my work life to my Christian life. So I find it valuable for many reasons.*

Even Monica was surprised by what the EVP had become for some of the CSB employees. As she considered how the EVP had impacted her workload after the bank opened another branch she revisited this e-mail message again. Monica wondered whether she, too, was expected to align her personal and professional lives at CSB. Or was it okay for her to keep her personal values and beliefs to herself, not expressing them at work like Renee?

Others had also seen the success of the EVP. The United Way of Little City asked Monica if the EVP could volunteer for the summer's largest community fundraiser, the annual walk-a-thon. Monica reluctantly agreed, knowing that not everyone would willingly give their holiday weekend to participate. Monica observed, during the last year since the EVP had begun, employees with children were not always coming through on their commitments, leaving those employees without children to fill the gaps. Just last week, she had overheard Eric telling his coworker, "If I miss one more of my daughter's soccer games because of the EVP, my wife is going to kill me."

Monica was not pleased. How many soccer games had she missed? She was committed to the bank and had made sacrifices in her own personal life to make the EVP successful. What about Renee? Renee shared what great meaning the EVP had in her life. Sure, she was exhausted several times last year as the EVP grew, but she also believed that being a community banker wasn't for everyone. Maybe CSB wasn't the place for Eric. After all, CSB was different: it valued people before profits and community over corporatization. Volunteering was an important aspect of CSB, and if Eric—or anyone—was going to be successful here, he needed to embrace the EVP. Monica decided she would speak with Eric tomorrow.

KEY TERMS

Employee Volunteerism - an element of voluntarism in which groups of employees are intentionally engaged as volunteers outside their respective workplace on behalf of their specific workplace while in the service of a nonprofit organization or local community organization.

Organizational Commitment - an individual's psychological attachment to the organization.

Organizational Identification - the importance of the organization in the person's self-concept.

Philanthropic Overtime - the expectation of participation in an employee volunteer program on behalf of the employee and the employer in which the employee is not receiving financial benefit for his/her participation in the employee volunteer program.

DISCUSSION QUESTIONS

1. Why is the EVP so important to Bob?
2. What motivates employees to extend themselves in philanthropic overtime? Is employee participation in the EVP a reasonable expectation?
3. If service commitment is important to your supervisor, does it need to be important to you? Why or why not?
4. What are the consequences of *not* participating in the EVP? Are the consequences in the spirit of the EVP?
5. To what extent are EVPs likely to affect employee identification and commitment?
6. Given the inherent contradictions between nonprofit and for-profit organizations, do nonprofit organizations compromise their missions when they use corporate volunteer programs? Why or why not?
7. Is it possible to reconcile the differences between business efforts to volunteer in communities and to make a profit? Why or why not?

SUGGESTED READINGS

Cheney, G. (1983). The rhetoric of identification and the study of organizational communication. *Quarterly Journal of Speech, 69*, 143–158. doi: 10.1080/00335638309383643

Coles, R. (1993). *The call of service: A witness to idealism.* New York, NY: Houghton Mifflin.

Freedman, M. (1993). *The kindness of strangers: Adult mentors, urban youth, and the new volunteerism.* San Francisco, CA: Jossey-Bass.

Hunt, S. D., & Morgan, R. M. (1994). Organizational commitment: One of many commitments or key mediating construct? *Academy of Management Journal, 37*, 1568–1587. doi: 10.2307/256799

Satterlund, A. M., (2004). *A thousand hours of overtime: A study of employee identification and commitment* (unpublished doctoral dissertation). University of North Carolina at Chapel Hill.

KEYWORDS

employee volunteerism, philanthropic overtime, organizational identification, organizational commitment

*This case study is based on dissertation research conducted by the first author. The events and conversations included in the case study are representative of data gathered from observations and interviews at a new community bank that had begun an employee volunteerism program.

CHAPTER TWENTY-FOUR

Discursive Closure IN Workplace Giving

Is There a Better Way to Encourage Charitableness at Work?*

JENNIFER MIZE SMITH

Western Kentucky University

Johnson was packing up his laptop to head home when the phone rang. It was nearly 6:00 p.m. on Friday. The bank had closed an hour ago, and he suspected he was the only one left in the building. He glanced at the caller ID; it was Jan, one of the branch managers across town. "If only I'd walked out the door five minutes earlier," he thought. As he contemplated whether or not to answer, he caught a glimpse of the shiny, brass nameplate on his desk—Vice President of Retail. He was Jan's direct supervisor. He really should see what she needed.

"Hello, this is Johnson," he said in his most pleasant voice.

"Hi, Johnson. It's Jan at the Eastside branch. I know it's late on a Friday afternoon, and I don't want to keep you," Jan continued. "I meant to call sooner but got busy with the Friday drive-thru traffic and didn't get a chance. I was wondering if we could get together on Monday morning. Maybe 9:00 a.m.? I'd like to discuss the United Way campaign instructions that branch managers were given today."

Johnson wanted to say he was busy, but his conscience got the better of him. "Sure," he said before giving himself time to change his mind. "I have a 10:00 a.m. meeting on that side of town, so I'll swing by your branch at 9:00. See ya then," he said, punching the date into his smartphone.

"Thanks," Jan replied. "Have a nice weekend."

****

On Monday morning, Johnson was knee-deep in quarterly reports when his phone beeped, alerting him of an appointment on his calendar—Jan at 9:00 a.m. He grabbed his suit jacket and started to his car.

On the drive across town, Johnson thought about his colleague Jan. They had both started on the teller line nearly 12 years ago and had gone through many training workshops together. Johnson had climbed the corporate ladder faster, although he wasn't sure why. Jan was smart and a go-getter, always prepared at meetings. She was compassionate yet firm with her subordinates and seemed to enjoy collaborating with others to solve problems. Johnson had often wondered why he continued to get promotions, while Jan seemed to stall at the level of branch manager. She wasn't afraid to raise issues, ask questions, or challenge decisions, but always professional and with good intentions. Johnson wished he was a bit more like her in that regard. "Perhaps she comes across too aggressive to some folks," he thought.

HONK! HONK! Johnson's thoughts were quickly interrupted by the blaring horn of the driver behind him. Startled, he looked up to see the traffic light had turned green. He shook his head, cleared his mind, and soon found himself at Jan's door.

"Hi, Johnson," said Jan, greeting him as he entered the branch lobby. "Come on in. I was just about to get us some coffee, and we can chat in my office."

"Sure thing," Johnson replied and followed her down a short, narrow hallway. He always enjoyed visiting the branches. It let him get out of the downtown highrise of Southern Bank's central office where he was housed, but, most importantly, he was reminded of the good work that the frontline tellers did every day. They were the face of the bank in the eyes of the public. He got caught up in watching a couple of them interact with customers and jumped when Jan said, "Okay, ready to get started?"

Jan sat down at a small meeting table in the corner of her office and motioned to a chair for Johnson. After a brief silence, she started. "You know, Johnson, I don't want to become a broken record about this charitable giving thing. I swear it's not that I'm *not* a charitable person. I don't want you to think *that*. I give to all kinds of things—St. Jude's Hospital, March of Dimes, arthritis research, and local places, too, like my church and the food pantry. I'm just not always comfortable with how charitable giving is done around here."

"I understand," Johnson replied, recalling having heard this introduction before. "So is there something specific you want to discuss?" he asked, waiting to learn of her latest concern.

"Well, after the United Way kickoff last Friday, we, the branch managers, were given a packet of materials detailing the campaign process. We're supposed to do all these promotions to get our employees to participate. 'We want 100% participation,' they kept saying. Now, I know United Way is a good cause and everything, and I know Kyle (the bank president) is real big on it, but I just don't agree with some of the things they're asking me to do."

Johnson set his coffee cup on the table and leaned back in his chair. "What kinds of things, Jan? I can't imagine anyone is asking you to do anything too bad if we're supposed to be raising money for something good," he said with a smile.

"I know, but, for example, there's going to be a competition among all the branches, and there are all these employee incentives for giving," she explained.

"Sounds like it could be fun, Jan. Could even be good for employee morale," Johnson interjected.

"Maybe, but it also creates pressure," Jan said.

"Pressure?" Johnson asked. "You're the only one who sees how much employees give. How is that pressure? Employees can give or not give. It's not like they're going to get punished if they don't. We're not going to fire them," Johnson said with a slight chuckle.

"That's just it!" Jan exclaimed. "They say everything is anonymous, but it's not. It can't be! If Susie gave the amount required to earn an extra vacation day, that day has to get scheduled and posted on the board. We're a small operation, so we have to discuss who is off when and how that shift will get covered. Everyone may not know exactly how much Susie gave, but they would all have an idea. If Lois can't give that much and doesn't get the extra day off, that'll get noticed, too. And if our branch isn't listed in the newsletter for having 100% participation, don't think people won't talk to try and figure out who didn't give."

Johnson was quiet, taking it all in. He hadn't thought of it that way.

"In all honesty," Jan continued, "I have some part-timers who should probably be *receiving* services from United Way. It'll be hard for them to participate, and I just don't feel right pushing all of these promotions on them or creating unnecessary discomfort among coworkers. But if my branch doesn't participate, then how will that look on me? Like I'm not charitable? Like I'm not a team player?"

Johnson had never known Jan to worry about what others thought of her. After a few seconds of silence, he asked, "Have you thought about talking with Kyle about this? Maybe he doesn't realize the position you're in."

"Yes," Jan replied. "I thought about going to him because I know he's the United Way board chair this year. But then I reread his letter in the promotion packet." She slid it across the table.

Johnson's eyes were immediately drawn to the last paragraph, highlighted in yellow, which read:

> *If for some reason you don't feel as strongly about this campaign as I do, please come talk to me, and I can give you specific examples of how we've seen United Way work … I hope to be able to make you feel differently after our conversation. – Kyle*

"Does that sound like an open door for discussion to you?" Jan snickered with a slight grin. "I've had similar concerns in the past, you know, about expecting our folks to make charitable donations at work. But the few comments I've made to him before, he's so into it … it's like talking to a wall," she said with a sigh.

Johnson nodded in agreement and promised to give it some thought. Jan had made some good points, but he wasn't sure how to address them. Everyone knew that United Way was the bank president's pet charity. Jan was right; it would be difficult to talk to him. Still, Johnson appreciated that Jan was looking out for her employees' feelings.

Back at the office, Johnson couldn't help but wonder if other bank employees shared Jan's concerns. As he entered the first floor, he passed Patty on the teller line. The building's three floors were mostly occupied by bank management and regional offices, but the first floor was home to the bank's largest branch operation. After some cordial chitchat, Johnson asked if their branch team would be participating in the United Way campaign.

"Of course!" Patty quickly replied. "You know, we get a free lunch at a nice restaurant if everyone gives at least $1! Guess that means you'll be coming downstairs to cover the drive-thru for me, eh?" She laughed, nudging him with her elbow.

"Yep, maybe I will," Johnson said, smiling. "So what do you think about us having the United Way campaign every year anyway?"

"I guess it's fine with me," Patty said. "I try to help out others if I can, but I don't know that much about charities. I figure there's probably people up there smarter than me. Most companies know where their money's going, and they wouldn't surely be just giving it to somebody who wasn't using it properly."

"Oh, it's a good cause," Johnson said. "I mean, there are lots of good causes, but United Way is certainly one of them. Hope you all get that free lunch!" he said and walked upstairs.

He saw Sam's door open. He rapped his knuckles across the doorplate, which read, "Vice President of Lending," and stuck his head in. "Got a minute?" he asked.

Sam looked up from his computer and said, "Sure, always for you, buddy. What's up?"

"Had an interesting conversation with Jan over at Eastside this morning, about this whole United Way thing," Johnson started.

"Not that again," sighed Sam. "Wasn't she the one who complained about adopting the family at Christmas?"

"Well, she didn't really complain," Johnson explained in her defense. "She just made a suggestion to improve the process. Instead of assigning items for each person to purchase, she thought it would be better for employees if they just pooled their money anonymously and then went shopping for supplies. You know, so it didn't create a hardship for someone who might be strapped for cash during the holidays. Anyway," he continued, "what do you think about asking employees to make a donation to United Way?"

"I think anyone who works here a while knows it's just part of the job. Me? I do the payroll deduction. It's like throwaway money, comes right off the top. I don't ever see it, and neither does my wife. Every year, we get those donation cards; I mark an amount, hand it to my secretary, and it's gone. I don't even think about how much it is," Sam said. "Besides," he continued, "everyone expects banks to be community minded these days, so we have to do *something* that looks good to the public."

"Don't get me wrong," Johnson began. "I'm not against charitable giving or anything. I even think it's good for employers to talk about giving and volunteering at work. Some people have to be encouraged to be charitable. I'm just wondering if there is a better way to go about it. You know, a more democratic process. Should employees be more involved in deciding who they support and how?"

Just then, the phone rang. Sam answered, paused, and whispered that he needed to take the call. Johnson nodded and headed for his office. There had to be a way to do workplace giving better, still supporting good causes but letting employees have more choice. But how?

KEY TERMS

Discursive Closure - the intentional or unintentional suppression of a particular conflict; active processes of discursive closure lead to and sustain systematically distorted communication.

Discursive Openings - opportunities for productive change where interests of multiple stakeholders are represented.

Employee Participation - organizational structures and processes that empower employees, give them a voice, and allow them to participate in decision making; the democratization of work processes.

Systematically Distorted Communication - when organizational procedures, policies, and rights of participation are continually reproduced by a dominant power and unable to be questioned by particular stakeholders.

Workplace Giving - when an employer provides an opportunity for, and sometimes expects, an employee to give time and/or money to a particular charity.

DISCUSSION QUESTIONS

1. To what extent are Jan's concerns about the campaign process founded?
2. What factors may have led to systematically distorted communication regarding the topic of charitable giving at the bank? How might the bank president's personal values have influenced the distortion?

3. Deetz (1992) outlined multiple discursive closure tactics. Provide examples from the case that illustrate the following:
   a. Disqualification—socially producing notions of expertise
   b. Legitimation—rationalizing decisions to make managerial practices appear acceptable and legitimate
   c. Naturalization—accepting a claim or practice as the taken-for-granted way it is
   d. Topical avoidance—prohibiting the discussion of some events and feelings, particularly areas of potential conflict

4. Why would most employees accept management-constructed ideas about charitable giving? How might Johnson create some discursive openings about charitable giving at work?

5. What might workplace giving at the bank look like if more employees participated in the decision-making process? How could employees have more voice in the process of choosing the charities they support?

6. If workplace giving at the bank was more democratized, how might the change in process affect the employees? United Way? Or other charitable organizations? What are the advantages and disadvantages of employee participation?

7. How would you advise Johnson to proceed—specifically, to address the concerns raised by Jan and more generally, to improve the process of workplace giving at the bank?

SUGGESTED READINGS

Deetz, S. A. (1992). *Democracy in an age of corporate colonization: Developments in communication and the politics of everyday life.* Albany, NY: SUNY Press.

Mize Smith, J. (2012). All good works are not created equal: Employee sensemaking of corporate philanthropy. *Southern Communication Journal, 77,* 369–388. doi: 10.1080/1041794X.2012.680796

Mize Smith, J., & Sypher, B. D. (2010). Philanthropy in the workplace: How a financial institution communicates charitable giving values [Special qualitative issue]. *Southern Communication Journal, 75,* 370–391. doi: 10.1080/1041794x.2010.504449

Stohl, C., & Cheney, G. (2001). Participatory processes/paradoxical practices: Communication and the dilemmas of organizational democracy. *Management Communication Quarterly, 14,* 349–407. doi: 10.1177/0893318901143001

Thackaberry, J. A. (2004). "Discursive opening" and closing in organizational self-study: Culture as trap and tool in wildland firefighting safety. *Management Communication Quarterly, 17,* 319–359. doi: 10.1177/0893318903259402

KEYWORDS

workplace giving, systematically distorted communication, discursive closure, discursive opening, employee participation

*This case is based on interview data with bank employees who were asked about charitable giving at work. Although the research was not focused on United Way, most participants cited examples from the United Way campaign as they described managerial constructions of giving and the lack of employee participation in decisions about workplace giving.

Client Connections: Serving Stigmatized Out-Groups

CHAPTER TWENTY-FIVE

Social Media AND Online Gaming

Strengthening Ties between Donors and Clients*

HOLLY J. PAYNE, JENNIFER MIZE SMITH, AND GANER L. NEWMAN IV

Western Kentucky University

As the new director of fundraising at A Way Forward, Inc. (AWF), a nonprofit organization dedicated to assisting individuals living below the poverty level, Colleen Wilson was charged with expanding their donor and volunteer base. AWF's mission was to provide food, clothing, and supportive services to homeless and indigent individuals. The organization worked to identify clients living below the poverty level who needed financial assistance and who were interested in seeking employment opportunities. Colleen's work with AWF and other nonprofit organizations had taught her that the plight of the homeless and of those living below the poverty level was often not readily recognizable, and so part of her challenge was educating her community about the level of need. Her review of contributor profiles indicated the organization had not done a very good job of cultivating relationships with the 18–30-year-old age group. Knowing this group to be an untapped resource, she set out to develop a research-based proposal to bring forward to the Board of Directors.

COLLEEN'S RESEARCH

Identification and NPOs

Colleen knew that she had to somehow connect potential donors and volunteers to the working poor who made up a large portion of AWF's client base. So she began her research by looking through notes from a course she took in organizational communication that focused on how people identify with organizations and their products or services. Identification, in its broadest sense, is widely understood as the perception of oneness or belongingness to a social group. Colleen read research to support what she already knew from her 10 years of nonprofit experience. The more individuals identify with a nonprofit, the more likely they are to give of their time and resources.

Increased patterns of giving and volunteering among those most identified with a nonprofit organization were not surprising. As Colleen reflected on the most active volunteers and donors at AWF, they seemed to feel a sense of connection to one another, to the staff, and to the organization. Perhaps more importantly, they seemed to feel connected to the clients. Colleen recalled hearing stories from volunteers and donors who explained that they, themselves, once had been only a few paychecks away from the situations of those they were serving. Again, Colleen's suspicions were confirmed in a book she read in her communication course. Individuals are more likely to donate to causes that help individuals who are perceived as being similar to them.

It was clear. Connecting potential volunteers and donors to AWF's clients was the key, but how? Colleen had seen many nonprofit campaigns focus on guilt-inducing messages but she was not convinced that strategy would work, particularly for reaching younger generations. Colleen was sure she needed to develop appeals of a different format.

COLLEEN'S STRATEGY

Social Media, Gaming, and NPOs

As Colleen pondered how to reach younger volunteers, she immediately thought about the use of online interactive media. She walked down the hall for a quick check of her instincts. She found AWF's two interns from the regional university's communication department and asked them two main questions: (1) How do you typically find out about a nonprofit organization? and (2) How would you show your support for a nonprofit organization?

As expected, the conversation turned to social media. The two college students explained that they would most likely pay attention to nonprofit causes if they were promoted by someone in their social network. In turn, they would show their support for a nonprofit by "liking" their page, posting links, and encouraging others to do the same.

Their responses were just as Colleen had thought. Yet she knew that AWF was not taking full advantage of Facebook and other social networking sites in its efforts to cultivate relationships. She planned to launch a Facebook page for AWF along with Twitter, Pinterest, and Instagram accounts. The assistant director of marketing would be responsible for the creation and upkeep of the sites with key messages and pictures posted before, during, and after major events. But Colleen also knew that would not be enough. AWF needed something new and different, something interactive that would get the younger generation involved in AWF's cause.

Colleen's interest was piqued when she read about the use of social games and their popularity on Facebook. In an effort to adapt to recessionary shifts in donor trends, some nonprofits had turned to the online gaming industry to develop social games that in some way worked to teach others about their particular cause. Video games, in particular, may hold tremendous potential for nonprofits seeking to induce identification between potential stakeholders and their causes. Colleen was shocked to read in the paper that, according to the Entertainment Software Association, over 72 million American households play computer or video games, and in 2010 alone, consumer spending in the gaming industry reached over 25 billion dollars.

It seemed to Colleen that online games might have potential for connecting a nonprofit organization with a younger audience, but she was unclear how until she came across what was, for her, a new term—*serious games* or games designed with intended purposes beyond user entertainment. Essentially, serious games virtualize real-world events occurring outside the scope of user awareness and place those users in the shoes of marginalized others.

Colleen became more intrigued when she found a study that examined the game *Darfur Is Dying*, a serious game in which users assume the role of a Darfurian refugee. The intent of the game was to raise awareness of the conditions in Darfur by placing users in a simulated environment, having them forage for water and showing players messages about the fate of Darfurian refugees when they fail to "hide" from the military junta. The authors found that individuals who played the game exhibited a greater willingness to help the Darfurian people than those who watched the game being played or those who simply read the game's persuasive texts. "That's it!" Colleen thought, as she imagined the potential of using a serious game to both raise awareness and encourage support for AWF beyond traditional persuasive efforts. Such a strategy might also open the door to more donations from around the country.

Pilot Test Using the Game *Decisions*

Having conducted her research, Colleen was set on using a serious game as part of her new youth campaign; however, she knew that it might take more data to convince the board to pay for the $50,000 creation of an online game solely dedicated to the AWF cause. She decided to run a pilot test using a similar game called *Decisions*. *Decisions* was an online game designed to educate and encourage donations for nonprofit organizations by placing the user in the metaphorical shoes of a working-poor American. The game seeks to subvert negative assumptions about homelessness by allowing gamers to virtually experience challenges faced by low-income individuals.

Decisions was developed by an advertising agency for the nonprofit organization Life Ministries of San Diego (LMSD). The game was designed to help LMSD solicit new volunteers and donors by encouraging players to experience the challenges facing the working poor. The hope was that after playing the game, participants would understand the difficult position of the working poor and be motivated to contribute.

Once users enter the *Decisions* website, they are told that they have lost their savings and their house and that they must make it through the month with only $1,000. The game then presents typical life occurrences and situations that any person might experience. Every day of the month, the user faces a series of challenges and is forced to make decisions, ranging from choosing a place to live to deciding whether or not to take a day off work to watch their child in the school play. Each decision has direct or indirect financial repercussions. In general, the most positive moral decisions are also the most costly, encouraging users to experience the dissonance associated with difficult choices. When users face certain decisions, one option is to "ask a friend," which links the user to their Facebook account and posts the request on a friend's wall. At the game's conclusion, whether or not the user "survived" the month, s/he is asked to either "Donate to LSMD," "Get Involved," or "Play Again." The "Donate to LMSD" option takes users to a PayPal page, while clicking "Get Involved" directs the user to the LMSD website. Colleen decided the best way to test the success of *Decisions* was to solicit participants to play the game and to examine the relationships between playing the game and their levels of identification, donation, and volunteering.

Colleen's Pilot Test Results

The AWF college interns were completing a research methods course and agreed to conduct the pilot study as part of their project. They solicited 55 undergraduate and graduate students to complete a survey of their identification level with the working poor, as well as their likelihood of donating and volunteering with AWF. The pilot test was set up as a pre/posttest design, so the participants completed the survey, played the game *Decisions*, and took the survey again. After the pre-test, the participants were divided into two groups, those with low levels of identification and those with high levels of identification in relation to the working poor.

Following the posttest, statistical analysis indicated that the game had no effect on participants who initially had high levels of identification with the working poor. What was interesting, however, was that those with low levels of identification with the working poor reported significantly higher levels of identification after playing the game. The second part of the analysis looked at whether there was a correlation between playing the game and donating money, volunteering, and "liking" the game on Facebook for others to see. There were significant relationships between participants' levels of identification with the working poor and their likelihood of donating time and money. Interestingly, however, they found a significant negative relationship between identification and the decision to "share" the game on Facebook.

Based on these results, Colleen felt strongly about the connection between identification and the game *Decisions,* and she was optimistic about the related outcomes, such as giving money and volunteering; however, she was less clear about why participants chose not to "like" the game on Facebook. She hoped this would not be a stumbling block in the Board of Directors' decision about funding the game. Perhaps she would just not mention that particular finding.

KEY TERMS

Identification - the perception of oneness or belongingness to a social group.

Organizational Identification - the perception of oneness or belongingness to an organization that includes emotional and motivational components.

Out-Groups - groups with which individuals do not perceive a shared social identity.

Social Information Processing Theory - describes how perceptions and relationships are formed in the online environment and how features of technology can aid in the development of attraction.

Social Identity Model of Deindividuation Effects (SIDE) - a model that describes how reduced nonverbal cues in computer-mediated environments cause individuals to cling to information from others about their social identities, causing exaggerated judgments.

DISCUSSION QUESTIONS

1. How does identifying with an out-group, such as the working poor or the homeless, differ from and/or connect with the concept of identifying with an organization? Describe ways NPOs can benefit from both.

2. How might identification with members of an out-group, such as the working poor, differ from identification with groups that might be considered less sympathetic, such as drug abusers or people who are HIV positive? Would NPO strategies differ based on the group in need?

3. In what ways can NPOs use social networking to attract donors and volunteers? Compare and contrast the persuasive elements of social media and face-to-face interactions.

4. In Colleen's pilot study, why do you think there was not a relationship between the participant's identification and their likelihood of sharing or "liking" the game on Facebook? How might social media behavior patterns influence this act? Consider Social Information Processing (SIP) theory, which explains social elements of technology use or the Social Identity Model of Deindividuation Effects (SIDE) theory, which speaks to identity and perceptions in the computer-mediated environment.

5. What ethical choices arise for Colleen as she prepares her presentation for the board? Should she share all of the study's findings? Why or why not?

6. If you were playing an online game, what features would attract your attention and make you more likely to connect with nonprofit service recipients on an emotional level? Do you think that an online game has the potential to affect your likelihood of volunteering with a NPO? Why or why not?

7. NPOs make many critical decisions on whether to fund projects or initiatives designed to expand their ability to meet the needs of their clients. In this case study, Colleen relies on surveys and a pilot test; what other data sources could be helpful to AWF's Board of Directors? How might data be used to assess the success of a program?

8. Do you think there is merit in spending $50,000 to try to gain donors? What percent of overhead should an organization spend on such activities rather than on direct benefits to the people it serves? Why?

SUGGESTED READINGS

Ashforth, B. E., & Mael, F. (1989). Social identity theory and the organization. *Academy of Management Review, 14*, 20–39. doi: 10.5465/AMR.1989.4278999

Peng, W., Lee, M., & Heeter, C. (2010). The effects of a serious game on role-taking and willingness to help. *Journal of Communication, 60*, 723–742. doi: 10.1111/j.1460-2466.2010.01511.x

Sargeant, A. (1999). Charitable giving: Towards a model of donor behavior. *Journal of Marketing Management, 15*, 215–238. doi: 10.1362/026725799784870351

Tidwell, M. V. (2005). A social identity model of prosocial behaviors within nonprofit organizations. *Nonprofit Management & Leadership, 15*, 449–467. doi: 10.1002/nml.82

KEYWORDS

organizational identification, out-groups, serious games, online gaming

*This case study is based on research that focused on the development of a new scale called the Identification with Perceived Out-Groups Scale (IPOGS). Although the characters and scenario in this case are fictitious, the scale was tested with a real online serious game called *Spent* found at http://www.gamesforchange.org/play/spent/. Scale development is ongoing and has led to additional studies presented at the Southern States Communication Association conference.

CHAPTER TWENTY-SIX

Volunteering WITH THE Unemployed IN THE Age-Old Search FOR Work*

ANGELA N. GIST

University of Kansas

Erwin had been trying to shake this slump forever. Ever since he lost his job as procurement specialist at Cornerstone Architecture and Development, he hadn't been the same. For 18 months, Erwin looked everywhere but still couldn't find work. He joined Executive Career Transitions (ECT) over a year ago to help with his job search, but so far things hadn't changed much. Just as Erwin pulled into the parking lot, he realized he was right behind Johnny. Johnny and Erwin had joined ECT at the same time. That seemed like such a long time ago. Now they had both become regulars.

Johnny greeted Erwin as they got out of their cars and walked into the ECT meeting together. "Hey, Erwin, how was your weekend?" he asked.

Erwin responded, "Not bad for an old-timer like me. I spent time with the grandkids so my son and his wife could take a weekend getaway for their anniversary."

Johnny replied, "That's nice. I didn't do much myself, just looked for work, as usual." Erwin and Johnny walked into the building, grabbed their name tags, settled in, and waited for things to get started. Johnny went to get a cup of coffee, and Erwin reflected back on his very first ECT meeting.

When Erwin first joined, ECT had 250 members. There were so many unemployed people in attendance that ECT moved the meeting to a gymnasium at a local church. Erwin heard about the meeting from Charlie, a former coworker, who was also laid off from Cornerstone. When they walked into the gymnasium,

Erwin and Charlie saw several others who had been laid off from their company. They all sat together.

Charlie said to Erwin and the others, "Look around, guys. What's the average age of everybody in this room?" They all agreed it was somewhere around 55 and wondered if their age had anything to do with getting laid off. Erwin thought it was crazy that he'd worked hard all his life, earned several promotions, learned his job, increased his skills, and ultimately priced himself out of the market. He knew he'd never make the money he was making at his last job. At this point, he was desperate to find work. Erwin hated that over time he'd become a staple member at ECT. So many others came, listened to the seminars, found jobs, volunteered at a few meetings, and left ECT. It hadn't worked that way for Erwin. One recruiter told Erwin companies were afraid to hire him because they couldn't pay him what he was worth. Erwin sighed audibly and then snapped back to reality. He realized the meeting was beginning.

Bob, president of ECT, started the meeting by introducing himself and the organization's mission. "Welcome to Executive Career Transitions. We are an organization committed to helping you during your career transition. I'm Bob Wilson, the president. I'm also an alum of ECT. That's right. I was in your shoes once and this organization helped me through my job search. I'm retired now and serve as president, so they pay me the big bucks." Everyone laughed at Bob's joke. "Just kidding. I'm a volunteer. In fact, ECT is run by volunteers. We're committed to volunteering here, and our goal is zero membership. We want you to find work. And we want you to know that ECT's goal is to get rid of you by helping you in your job search. So to all the newcomers and returning members, we're happy to have you, but sorry to see you here because we know that means you're in between jobs. I'm going to turn it over to our guest presenter, Dane Birsch. Dane is one of the strongest corporate recruiters in the city." Everyone applauded as Dane stood up and walked toward the front.

The title of Dane's PowerPoint presentation was *What's Going on in the Job Market?* "Hi, I'm Dane. I specialize in recruitment and placement for senior-level professionals at all the major corporations headquartered here. Based on my expertise and the experiences of my clients, I'm going to share with you a few trends that are impacting the job market and your search for work. First, we'll talk about social networking online. Then we'll move on to how automation and technological advancements are impacting various industries. Now, I'll be honest. You're not the people I'm typically recruiting. I only recruit people who are actually working. But I'll still take your information, and once you're working, then I can help. My biggest piece of advice is that you take any job you can get because you're five times more employable once you have a job. If you settle, just know the job you take is a one-night stand, not a marriage. Anyway, I digress. Let's move on. We're going to start with a quick video …"

Dane's words came over the ECT members like a dark cloud. The whole mood in the room shifted. Why would Dane even come to ECT if he wasn't willing to help unemployed people? Erwin's shoulders slumped as he thought to himself. He didn't want to take just any job. He'd become an expert in his industry. And how dare they bring in a speaker who didn't want to work with the unemployed. Wasn't that the whole goal of ECT?

Dane's presentation was discouraging at best. He talked about how automation of certain business practices eliminated jobs and how job postings and networking had migrated online. Dane said all industries were looking for employees who were on the cutting edge of technology. Erwin was 64 years old. He knew his industry well, but he would never be on the cutting edge of technology. Dane's words reminded Erwin of a few guys he worked with back at Cornerstone.

Erwin raised his hand and Dane acknowledged him. "At least once a month, I get a call from a past coworker that got laid off. We're talking about architects and engineers. One is going to try to sell real estate now. The other one, he said he's had to learn his craft three times. He learned it in architecture school with pencil, paper, T-squares, and triangles. Then CAD came along, computer-aided design, had to learn that. Now it's RIM and BIM and all this other stuff. So, I think I'm a dinosaur. I'm out of the …" Erwin felt his eyes welling up with tears as he paused for a moment. "The one guy, he's getting out of it. He said he learned it on pencil and paper. The kids coming out of school now, they're all computer geeks. They pick this stuff up."

Another ECT member chimed in after Erwin. "How do I compete with my 22-year-old son on the job market?" The room grew silent.

Dane paused and then carefully replied, "You *can* compete, but you have to understand while you're not on the cutting edge of technology, you *are* on the cutting edge of business understanding and know-how. That's what you bring to the table." That was the first encouraging thing Dane had said. Erwin knew the truth that there was a wealth of experience in that room. While Erwin felt like a dinosaur, he refused to believe that he was set out to pasture. Erwin felt he had a lot to offer. It was true that most ECT members had more than a decade of industry experience. But their experience came with age because they all put in the time to develop professional expertise. Dane continued with his presentation. At the end, the meeting opened up for questions and comments.

Kerry Rousch, another member of ECT, spoke up. "I have a dilemma. I went to college for a year and a half and then dropped out because I had my daughter. After I raised her, I went back to school and finished my associates' degree in applied science. I worked as an RN for 11 years. Then I had to leave work again to take care of my mom, who passed away last year. But now all I can find is part-time work. I'm ready to work full-time again. I've always worked. I'm not lazy. But juggling part-time jobs isn't paying the bills. I'm in my mid-40s, and I was a good nurse. I feel like I should be more marketable. I mean, I've got experience. I've finished my child rearing, and I'm single. I'm a divorced empty nester. I'm an ideal worker. But I feel like these people are only hiring new RNs, you know, graduates, over me, which doesn't make sense because they need training. Everybody says they need more nurses, but I can't find work."

Erwin chimed in. "I'm in a similar situation. I've been unemployed for 18 months. I've searched everywhere. I've been told I'm overqualified. I tell them it doesn't matter, that I'll do anything to provide for my family. But I can't even get an interview." There was a bit of silence in the room. Kerry's and Erwin's situations were similar to what many ECT members were struggling with during their job searches.

Dane offered advice. "The tough reality, folks, is that you need to be more strategic about your age. It's working against you. The odds are you're going to interview with a different generation from you, a younger generation. And you have to learn how to conceal your age because other people can't see the value you're bringing to the company. Hiring managers see you as someone who's past their prime. One way you can hide your age is by changing your résumé. Take off graduation dates and some of your earlier positions."

Dane's advice frustrated Johnny. He had heard this advice before and disagreed with it. "I've been given a lot of tips about hiding my age. And you can find lots of tricks about it online, too. I mean, if we're honest about it, we're not the greenest bunch of people I've ever seen. But the truth is … I don't want to hide my age. And honestly, I've heard it the other way, too. One career coach told me, 'Oh no, we want experience. Share it all.' Quite frankly, it's a good thing that I haven't missed one day of work in the last 17 years. I go to work, and I'm not late. I'm dependable. My résumé has everything from when I graduated high school to what I did at my last position because … I think that everything I've done has led to who I am now. All my experiences mean I have a lot to offer to a future employer. It's just my opinion, but I really don't want to hide my age." Johnny's commentary stirred a bit of energy in the room. People started nodding and making comments to their neighbors.

After the room quieted a bit, Scott, the volunteer executive director, stood and said, "Well, folks, we're nearly out of time. But I think we've hit on some important issues. The harsh reality is you're out of work, and it isn't fair, but the job market doesn't work in our favor. You should all strongly consider some of the suggestions Dane shared about concealing your age. Don't let your pride keep you from missing out on a great opportunity simply because you don't want to remove a date or two from your résumé. It's just something to think about. Our presentation for next week is titled, 'Rebound: Seven Steps for Coping with Change and Grieving Your Job Loss.' Thanks for coming out, and we'll see you next week."

The meeting was adjourned. Erwin left the meeting feeling at a loss. He didn't know what to do, but he knew he needed work.

KEY TERMS

Ageism - systematic stereotyping and discrimination against people because of age (Allen, 2011).

Metamorphosis Phase - one phase of the assimilation process that occurs when an organizational member is no longer a newcomer and has become established in the organization by making the transition from organizational outsider to insider (Kramer, 2010).

Organizational Assimilation - the processes (including forms of communication) by which individuals join, participate in, and leave organizations (Kramer, 2010).

Stigma - discrediting mark on one's identity that is spread through communication (Meisenbach, 2010; Smith, 2007).

DISCUSSION QUESTIONS

Organizational Assimilation: Recruitment and Retention

1. How is the goal of reaching zero membership different than typical organizational membership goals?
2. How does communication change at an organization when it is undesirable for service recipients to reach the metamorphosis phase of organizational assimilation through long-term membership? What types of things were said at ECT that revealed short-term membership as desirable?
3. What other types of nonprofit organizations should aim to have low or short-term membership (e.g., grief support groups, cancer support groups, etc.)? How can these types of nonprofit organizations help their members avoid reaching the metamorphosis phase of organizational assimilation (i.e., becoming established regulars)?
4. What other types of nonprofit organizations might recruit alumni members to volunteer once they've moved past traditional organizational membership (e.g., alcoholics/narcotics anonymous, sororities/fraternities)?
5. How might alumni volunteering change the organizational experience compared with volunteers who have had no prior history with the nonprofit organization? What are the advantages/disadvantages of having past service beneficiaries come back to volunteer with that nonprofit organization?

Stigma

6. Why are middle-aged and unemployed people stigmatized in society? Do ECT volunteers help its members navigate a job market full of stigma/discrimination? Or are ECT's messages perpetuating age and unemployment stigma/discrimination? Why or why not?
7. How might doing volunteer work be a viable way to get back into employment?
8. Volunteers commonly serve stigmatized populations (e.g., food bank, homeless shelters, etc.). What is the role of nonprofit organizations in helping remove societal stigmas and stereotypes?

SUGGESTED READINGS

Allan, P. (1990). Looking for work after forty: Job search experiences of older unemployment managers and professionals. *Journal of Employment Counseling, 27*, 113–121. doi: 10.1002/j.2161-1920.1990.tb00370.x

Allen, B. J. (2011). *Difference matters: Communicating social identity.* Long Grove, IL: Waveland Press.

Kramer, M. W. (2010). *Organizational socialization: Joining and leaving organizations.* Malden, MA: Polity Press.

Meisenbach, R. J. (2010). Stigma management communication: A theory and agenda for applied research on how individuals manage moments of stigmatized identity. *Journal of Applied Communication Research, 38*, 268–292. doi: 10.1080/00909882.2010.490841

Smith, R. A. (2007). Language of the lost: An explication of stigma communication. *Communication Theory, 17*, 462–485. doi: 10.1111/j.1468-2885.2007.00307.x

Trethewey, A. (2001). Reproducing and resisting the master narrative of decline: Midlife professional women's experiences of aging. *Management Communication Quarterly, 15*, 183–226. doi: 10.1177/0893318901152002

KEYWORDS

nonprofit support services, alumni volunteers, ageism, stigma, organizational assimilation, metamorphosis, unemployment

*This case study is based on research conducted for the author's dissertation research completed at the University of Missouri. The specific data that inform this case study come from ethnographic fieldwork and interview data collected at a nonprofit volunteer unemployment support organization. Names, situations, and facts have been changed to protect the privacy of individuals and organizations that agreed to volunteer for this research.

Author Biographies

Lindsey B. Anderson (Ph.D., Purdue University) is an assistant professor in the Department of Communication at the University of Maryland, College Park. She is interested in examining the intersections of communication, age, and emotion in the workplace. Her research has appeared in such outlets as the *Journal of Public Relations Review, Management Communication Quarterly, Communication Yearbook, Communication Research Reports*, and the *Journal of Professional Communication*. Lindsey can be reached at lbander@umd.edu.

Jane Stuart Baker (Ph.D., organizational communication, Texas A&M University) is an assistant professor in the Department of Communication at the University of Alabama. Her research focuses on organizational discourse, conflict, and group communication. Her recent work has appeared in *Research Methods for Studying Small Groups: A Behind-the-Scenes Guide* (Taylor & Francis, 2012), *Case Studies in Organizational Communication: Ethical Perspectives and Practices* (Sage, 2012), and *Reframing Difference in Organizational Communication Studies: Research, Pedagogy, and Practice* (Sage, 2011). She may be contacted at jsbaker@ua.edu.

Jessica Martin Carver (M.A., communication, Western Kentucky University) is a director of development for the College of Education and Behavioral Sciences at Western Kentucky University. She also teaches part-time in the Department of Communication. Her research focuses on both metaphors and tensions in higher education fundraising. This focus lead to a presentation at Southern States Communication Association Convention on her qualitative study dealing with metaphors in higher education development and a separate comprehensive thesis on metaphors and tensions within the profession of higher education fundraising. She has also presented at the Council for the Advancement and Support of Education's (CASE) Annual District III Conference and currently serves on the CASE Kentucky Conference planning committee.

Robin Patric Clair (Ph.D., Kent State University) is a full professor in the Brian Lamb School of Communication at Purdue University. Professor Clair's research interests include organizational communication, ethnography, rhetoric, and diversity issues. She has been a contributing researcher to the field of organizational communication for 25 years and has published in *Communication Monographs, Management Communication Quarterly, Journal of Applied Communication Research, Cultural Studies↔Critical Methodologies*, and many other journals. She is the author of four books and numerous articles. She has received two Outstanding Book of the Year awards, two Outstanding Research Article of the Year awards, several Top Paper awards, and the Golden Anniversary Award for her research. She has been named a Diversity Fellow as well as a Fellow to the Center of Artistic Endeavors and has published an organizationally-based novel—*Zombie Seed and the Butterfly Blues: A Case of Social Justice*, which deals with the development of GMOs. During the 2013/14 academic year, Professor Clair was inducted into the Book of Great Teachers at Purdue University. Professor Clair can be reached at rpclair@purdue.edu.

Suzy D'Enbeau (Ph.D., organizational communication, Purdue University) is an assistant professor in the School of Communication Studies at Kent State University. Her research explores how social change organizations navigate competing goals in domestic and transnational contexts; problematizes dominant ways of thinking about, constructing, and performing gender in different organizational contexts and in popular culture; and unpacks some of the challenges of qualitative inquiry in terms of analysis and researcher identity. In addition to numerous book chapters, her work has appeared in leading journals such as *Communication Monographs, Feminist Media Studies, Human Relations, Journal of Applied Communication Research, Qualitative Inquiry, Qualitative Communication Research*, and *Women's Studies in Communication*. Suzy can be reached at sdenbeau@kent.edu.

Kristina Drumheller (Ph.D., communication, University of Missouri-Columbia) is an associate professor of communication studies at West Texas A&M University. Her research interests include organizational rhetoric, crisis communication, media effects, and leadership. She is a principal in the collaborative research group Media Buffs, with research focusing on organizational crisis communication, mobile app trends, and consumer ethnocentric tendencies. Her work is published in journals such as *Communication Studies, Public Relations Review, Journal of Communication & Religion,* and *Speaker & Gavel.* She has won awards for her teaching and intellectual contributions and was the 2014 recipient of the WTAMU Social Justice Leadership award. She may be contacted at kdrumheller@wtamu.edu.

Kim Fletcher (M.A., sociology, Western Kentucky University) is a doctoral candidate at Kennesaw State University in the International Conflict Management program. Her primary research focuses on simulating and minimizing conflict vulnerability, and she is also interested in the use of sport in the reintegration of child soldiers and other peace-building processes. Her interest in organizational behavior and communication began while serving as a Peace Corps volunteer in Gambia from 2004 to 2006. Her current organizational research examines target selection and decision-making processes in NGO advocacy. She can be contacted at kfletch9@kennesaw.edu.

May Hongmei Gao (Ph.D., organizational communication, University of South Florida) is a professor of communication and Asian studies at Kennesaw State University in Atlanta. Dr. Gao is the founder and chair of the Symposium on ASIA-USA Partnership Opportunities (SAUPO), the largest Asia business conference in the South. *Georgia Asian Times* named her as one of the "25 Most Influential Asian Americans in Georgia (2013)." Dr. Gao has published over 25 articles in journals of communication, business, and Asian Studies. Her recent research focuses on intercultural adaptation of business models, social media communication, and mergers and acquisitions issues for multinational corporations. She can be reached at mgao@kennesaw.edu.

R. Nicholas Gerlich (Ph.D., marketing, Indiana University) is the Hickman Professor of Marketing at West Texas A&M University. His research focuses on social media, crisis communication, TV fandom, pop culture, historic roads and signage, and nonstore retailing. He is a principal in the collaborative research group Media Buffs with research focusing on marketing trends, consumer ethnocentric tendencies, and consumer behavior. He is currently working on a chapter on the economic impacts of filming *Breaking Bad.* His teaching areas include evolutionary marketing, marketing research, personal selling, and the principles class. Outside of class, his interests include cycling, photography, Route 66, and neon signs. He may be contacted at ngerlich@wtamu.edu.

Tamar Ginossar (Ph.D., University of New Mexico) is an assistant professor at the Department of Communication and Journalism at the University of New Mexico. Her research focuses on health communication in the context of culture and health disparities. Her research includes community and clinic-based mixed-methods examination of such communication in the context of cancer, HIV, and early childhood development and behavioral health. She is currently funded by the New Mexico Department of Health to conduct a statewide HIV services needs assessment in federally funded (Ryan White) clinics and agencies. Her articles were published in leading journals, including the *Journal of Applied Communication, Computer-Mediated Communication,* and *Health Communication.* She is also the lead author of six book chapters.

Angela N. Gist (Ph.D., organizational communication, University of Missouri) is an assistant professor in the Department of Communication Studies at the University of Kansas. She is an interpretive critical scholar who largely analyzes issues of social mobility and power. Her program of research emerges out of three areas of interest: social class, social identity, and organizational culture. Her most recent research analyzed the experiences of the unemployed across social class groups while they managed joblessness through organizational memberships. She also examines the identity work and negotiation of individuals' experiences as they cope with the absence of work and stigma. She may be contacted via e-mail at angela.gist@ku.edu.

Alan Hansen (Ph.D., sociology and communication, University at Albany, SUNY) is an associate professor in the Communication Department, Carroll College–Montana. His research touches areas related to intercultural communication, language and social interaction, membership categorization, identity, immigration, and ethnography. Dr. Hansen has published articles in *Research on Language and Social Interaction* and *Journal of Intercultural Communication,* and coauthored a chapter in *Telling Stories: Building Bridges among Language, Narrative, Identity, Interaction, Society, and Culture.* Before moving to Carroll College in Montana, he was a tenured associate professor at Texas A&M University-Corpus Christi. He may be contacted at ahansen@carroll.edu.

Timothy Huffman (Ph.D., human communication, Arizona State University) is an assistant professor in the Communication Studies Department at Loyola Marymount University. He studies socially just communication and focuses on topics like community, altruism, and compassion. He takes a participatory action, qualitative approach to research design and strives to help communities discover creative ways to improve organized action. He focuses especially on issues surrounding homelessness and partners with various nonprofits that provide outreach, permanent supportive housing, and other services. He may be contacted at timothy.huffman@lmu.edu.

Jessica Katz Jameson (Ph.D., communication, Temple University) is an associate professor in the Department of Communication at North Carolina State University. Her research in organizational communication focuses on conflict management, where she has made contributions to the study of mediation, emotion in conflict, and health communication. Her most current research program has focused on nonprofit Boards of Directors and communication practices that constitute generative governance. Her research has been published in journals such as the *Western Journal of Communication, International Journal of Conflict Management, Negotiation Journal,* and *Conflict Resolution Quarterly,* and she is currently working on a book on engaging conflict productively in organizations. She may be contacted at jameson@ncsu.edu.

Jeannette Kindred (Ph.D., communication, Wayne State University) is an associate professor of communication in the Department of Communication, Media and Theatre Arts at Eastern Michigan University. Her research has primarily focused on the scholarship of teaching and learning (in particular group learning, learning through case studies, and assessment of student learning gains via academic service learning [ASL] pedagogy) and university-community partnerships (specifically the impact of ASL on nonprofit organizations). Recent research activities include "Assessing Affective Learning via an Academic Service-Learning Capstone Course" (presentation, National Communication Association, 2013) and "Expectations versus Reality in a University-Community Partnership: A Case Study" (*Voluntas, International Journal of Voluntary and Nonprofit Organizations,* August 2014). She can be reached at jkindred@emich.edu.

Emily S. Kinsky (Ph.D., mass communications, Texas Tech University) serves as an assistant professor in the Department of Communication at West Texas A&M University. Her research interests include social media, crisis communication, and portrayals of public relations. In 2013, she received an award from the Sybil B. Harrington College of Fine Arts and Humanities for her intellectual contributions. She is the Vice Head Elect for the Public Relations Division of the Association for Education in Journalism and Mass Communication. She helps advise WTAMU's chapters of Public Relations Student Society of America, American Advertising Federation, and National Broadcasting Society. In March 2014, she was named national adviser of the year for NBS. She may be contacted at ekinsky@wtamu.edu.

Christopher J. Koenig (Ph.D., medical communication, University of California, Los Angeles) is an assistant professor in the Department of General Internal medicine at the University of California, San Francisco. His research emphasis is on the social dimensions of health and illness and emphasizes the mediating role of communication on the social, organizational, and cultural context of providing and receiving healthcare. His particular focus is the study of how language shapes communication by investigating communication as an interactive and social process. While his research typically uses empirical audiovisual recordings to apply the theory and method of conversation analysis, he has also published articles using diverse data sources, including interviews, focus groups, and participant observation, for interpretive and critical analyses. He may be contacted at christopher.koenig@ucsf.edu.

Michael W. Kramer (Ph.D., organizational communication, University of Texas) is professor and chair in the Department of Communication at the University of Oklahoma. His recent research has focused on volunteers, primarily in community theater productions and community choirs. In addition to this book, this work has led to two other books, *Volunteering and Communication: Studies from Multiple Contexts* (2013) and *Volunteering and Communication Volume 2: Studies in International and Intercultural Contexts* (2015). His other organizational research focuses on the assimilation/socialization processes of employee transitions such as newcomers, transfers, promotions, and exits. His group research focuses on decision making and leadership. He has made theoretical contributions in the theory of managing uncertainty (*Managing Uncertainty in Organizational Communication*, 2004) and group dialectical theory. He may be contacted at mkramer@ou.edu.

Sant Kumar (B.A., English and psychology, Occidental College) is a research assistant in the Vets Return Home Research Group at the San Francisco VA Medical Center. He is currently enrolled in the premedicine postbaccalaureate program at San Francisco State University. He may be contacted at sant.j.kumar@gmail.com.

Adrianne Kunkel (Ph.D., interpersonal communication, Purdue University) is a professor in the Department of Communication Studies at the University of Kansas. Her research focuses on emotional support/coping processes in personal relationships and support group settings, romantic relationship (re)definition processes, sex/gender similarities and differences, sexual harassment, and domestic violence intervention. Along with an edited book (2012), *Relationship Science: Integrating Evolutionary, Neuroscience, and Sociocultural Approaches*, and a coauthored book (2014), *Researching Interpersonal Relation-*

ships: Qualitative Methods, Studies, and Analysis, she has published multiple book chapters, along with several research articles in a variety of journals, including *Human Communication Research, Communication Monographs*, the *Journal of Applied Communication Research*, the *Journal of Social and Personal Relationships, Health Communication, Death Studies*, and the *Journal of Family Communication*. She may be contacted at adkunkel@ku.edu.

Murray W. Lee (M.Div., Covenant Theological Seminary) is a senior pastor at Cahaba Park Church in Birmingham, Alabama. He is currently a Ph.D. candidate at the University of Alabama in the school of Communication and Informational Sciences. His research interests lie in organizational communication, organizational identity and change, and leadership studies. He may be reached at mlee@cahabapark.org.

Joanne M. Marshall (Ed.D., administration, planning, and social policy, Harvard University) is an associate professor of educational administration at Iowa State University, where she serves as program coordinator. Her research agenda focuses on how people's internal values and beliefs relate to their public school roles, particularly in the areas of religion/spirituality, moral and ethical leadership, philanthropy, social justice pedagogy, and work-life balance. A former high school English teacher, she has published articles in the *Journal of School Leadership, Equity and Excellence in Education, Educational Administration Quarterly, School Administrator*, and *Phi Delta Kappan*. She is the lead editor of *Juggling Flaming Chainsaws: Faculty in Educational Leadership Try to Balance Work and Family* and editor of the Work-Life Balance book series from Information Age Publishing. Her website is http://www.public.iastate.edu/~jmars/.

Steven K. May (Ph.D., organizational communication, University of Utah) is an associate professor in the Department of Communication Studies at the University of North Carolina at Chapel Hill. His research interests include organizational ethics and corporate social responsibility, with particular attention to ethical practices of dialogue, transparency, participation, courage, and accountability. His edited books include *The Handbook of Communication Ethics, The Handbook of Communication and Corporate Social Responsibility, The Debate over Corporate Social Responsibility, Case Studies in Organizational Communication: Ethical Perspectives and Practices*, and *Engaging Organizational Communication Theory and Research: Multiple Perspectives*. His current book projects include *Corporate Social Responsibility: Virtue or Vice?* and *Working Identity*.

Kirstie McAllum (Ph.D., organizational communication, University of Waikato) is an assistant professor in the Département de communication at the Université de Montréal, Canada. Her research focuses on understanding how organizational members who do not interact regularly construct the meanings of their work as well as how persons who occupy hybrid public-private spaces construct organizational and occupational identities. She also investigates how discourses about professionalism combine with organizational control and co-ordination mechanisms to structure relationality in particular ways, often with the aim of increasing collaboration, and frequently of minimizing or suppressing dissent. Her work on volunteers and volunteering has been published in *Management Communication Quarterly* and *Communication Yearbook*. She may be contacted at kirstie.mcallum@umontreal.ca.

Lacy G. McNamee (Ph.D., University of Texas at Austin) is an assistant professor of organizational communication in Baylor University's Department of Communication. Her research focuses on organizational socialization and the negotiation of members' roles, responsibilities, and relationships. Her recent work has more specifically examined the communication dynamics between different member types in nonprofit and faith-based organizational settings, such as paid staff and volunteers. Lacy's work has been published in journals including *Communication Monographs, Management Communication Quarterly, Journal of Applied Communication Research, Health Communication,* and *Human Relations,* and she has served as a board director, adviser, and consultant for several nonprofit and volunteer-based organizations. Send correspondence to: Lacy_McNamee@baylor.edu.

Rebecca J. Meisenbach (Ph.D., organizational communication and public affairs issue management, Purdue University) is an associate professor in the Department of Communication at the University of Missouri and associate editor of the Americas for the journal *Culture and Organization*. She studies issues of identity and ethics, particularly in relation to nonprofit and gendered organizing. She is currently studying how working mothers manage the return to paid work after a maternity leave and how individuals manage nested and stigmatized identities. Recent examples of her research can be found in *Communication Monographs,* the *Journal of Applied Communication Research,* and *Management Communication Quarterly*. She may be contacted at meisenbachr@missouri.edu.

Trudy Milburn (Ph.D., communication, University of Massachusetts, Amherst) is an associate scholar with the Center for Local Strategies Research, University of Washington. Her research examines the discursive practices organizational and group members employ as they work to accomplish common goals. In addition to journal articles and chapters, Dr. Milburn explores these themes in her book, *Nonprofit Organizations: Creating Membership through Communication,* as well as her coauthored book, *Citizen Discourse on Contaminated Water, Superfund Cleanups, and Landscape Restoration: (Re)making Milltown, Montana.* She has been a tenured associate professor on the faculties of California State University Channel Islands and Baruch College/The City University of New York, and is a past chair of the Language and Social Interaction Division of the National Communication Association. She may be contacted at trudy.milburn2010@gmail.com.

Jennifer Mize Smith (Ph.D., organizational communication, Purdue University) is an associate professor in the Department of Communication at Western Kentucky University. Her research focuses on issues of identity and identification, corporate giving, fundraising rhetoric, and other communication processes in and of the nonprofit sector. She explores the ways in which giving and volunteering are socially constructed in various contexts (e.g., workplace, family, school, leisure) and the extent to which those meanings (re)construct one's philanthropic self. Her work has been published in the *International Journal of Business Communication*, the *Southern Communication Journal*, and *Communication Studies*, as well as the edited volumes of *Volunteering and Communication: Studies from Multiple Contexts* and *Volunteering and Communication Volume 2: Studies in International and Intercultural Contexts.* She may be contacted at jennifer.mize.smith@wku.edu.

Ganer L. Newman IV (M.A., organizational communication, Western Kentucky University) is the Director of Forensics at Western Kentucky University. His research interests involve the study of mechanisms designed to induce identification. He has written two books on public speaking: *Interpretation of Literature: Bringing Words to Life* (2013), published by the National Speech and Debate Association, and *Authentic Communication: Public Speaking for Everyone*, a high school public speaking textbook for the International Debate Education Association. He may be contacted at ganer.newman@wku.edu.

John G. Oetzel (Ph.D., University of Iowa), is a professor in the Department of Management Communication in the Waikato Management School at the University of Waikato in Hamilton, New Zealand. His research program focuses on understanding and improving challenging communication among people with different group identities (particularly cultural identities). He uses quantitative survey methods and/or mixed method designs to address 1) conflict in culturally diverse work groups and organisations, 2) communication in the health care delivery process, and 3) partnerships between community members and academics to address community health. He is co-author (with Stella Ting-Toomey) of *Managing Intercultural Communication Effectively* (2001) and co-editor (with Stella Ting-Toomey) of *The Sage Handbook of*

Conflict Communication (2006, 2013). He also authored *Intercultural Communication: A Layered Approach* (2009 and more than 80 articles/book chapters. He may be contacted at joetzel@waikato.ac.nz.

Holly J. Payne (Ph.D., communication, University of Kentucky) is an associate professor in the Department of Communication at Western Kentucky University. Her research focuses on dissent expression and communication competence in the organizational context. Her work in this area is published in *Communication Research Reports*, the *International Journal of Business Communication*, the *Journal of Leadership and Organizational Studies*, and *Employee Relations*. More recently, her research has focused on the impact of identification within the nonprofit sector as it relates to potential donors and volunteers and school crisis communication. In addition to scholarly journal articles, she is coauthor of *Competent Communication at Work: Strategies and Standards for Success* and is the current editor of the *Kentucky Journal of Communication*. She may be contacted at holly.payne@wku.edu.

Brittany L. Peterson (Ph.D., University of Texas at Austin) is an assistant professor in the School of Communication Studies and the Coordinator of E-Learning for the Scripps College of Communication at Ohio University. Her research focuses on challenging, deconstructing, and extending traditional understandings of membership in organizations with a specific focus on involuntary membership in and around correctional institutions and voluntary membership in "high-stakes" organizations (e.g., volunteer fire departments). Her scholarship is tied to socialization, identification, and structuration processes. She teaches graduate and undergraduate classes on organizational communication, socialization, membership, and interpretive research methods. Brittany's work has been published in peer-reviewed journals, including *Management Communication Quarterly, Communication Monographs, Communication Quarterly, Communication Education*, and *Journal of Applied Social Science*, as well as in edited books. Contact her at Brittany.Peterson.1@ohio.edu.

Claudia Petrescu (Ph.D. public policy and public administration, University of Pittsburgh) is a professor of public administration in the Department of Political Science at Eastern Michigan University. Her research focuses on nonprofit management, capacity building, strategic planning, organizational change, and evaluation. Securing grant funding, Dr. Petrescu contributed to the creation of the Institute for the Study of Children, Families, and Communities' Capacity Building Center (EMU) and to the creation of the EMU Nonprofit Leadership Alliance's (NLA) Student Funders Group. Dr. Petrescu's latest publications are "Expectations versus Reality in a

University-Community Partnership: A Case Study" (*Voluntas, International Journal of Voluntary and Nonprofit Organizations*, August 2014) and Are we better today than we were yesterday? Changes in leadership practices of nonprofit governing boards (*International Leadership Journal*, 2013). She can be reached at cpetrescu@emich.edu.

Jessica M. Rick (M.A., communication, North Dakota State University) is a doctoral student at the University of Missouri. Her organizational research addresses the communicative construction of identity, stigma, and work-family interactions. Current projects focus on: gender communication in engineering programs, nonprofit identification strategies, and work-parent boundaries. She is currently studying how workers navigate ideal work norms and parenthood. Her work has been published in the *Journal of Applied Communication Research* and the *Journal of General Education*. Jessica may be contacted at jessicarick@mizzou.edu.

Alysson M. Satterlund (Ph.D., interpersonal and organizational communication, University of North Carolina at Chapel Hill) currently serves as the senior assistant dean for Student Academic Support Services, director of the Office of Pluralism and Leadership, and the codirector of the Student Academic Support Center at Dartmouth College.

Sherianne Shuler (Ph.D., organizational communication, University of Kansas) is an associate professor of communication studies at Creighton University. Her research interests focus on the intersections of organizational communication and gender studies, as well as media representations of work-life. Research projects have involved the exploration of the emotional labor and coping strategies of such diverse groups as 911 dispatchers, domestic violence employees, patients facing a health crisis, and reference librarians. She has also published critiques of the portrayal of executive women in *Fortune* magazine and the depiction of women's friendships on *Desperate Housewives*. Her work has appeared in *Management Communication Quarterly, Health Communication, American Communication Journal, Women's Studies in Communication, Electronic Journal of Communication, Communication Studies*, and in several edited volumes. She can be contacted at sherishu@creighton.edu.

Stacy Tye-Williams (Ph.D., organizational communication, University of Nebraska-Lincoln) is an assistant professor of communication studies in the Department of English at Iowa State University. Her research focuses on how people narratively construct meaning in and about organizations. She examines dark- and bright-side processes in organization life, ranging from workplace bullying to the power of collective storytelling to bring about positive change. Her ultimate focus is how people use communication to organize and create positive outcomes in their organizations and the communities in which they are embedded. Along with several book chapters, she has published articles in *Management Communication Quarterly, Women and Language, Western Journal of Communication,* and *Communication Studies.* She may be contacted at styewill@iastate.edu.

Michelle T. Violanti (Ph.D., University of Kansas) is an associate professor in the School of Communication Studies at the University of Tennessee, Knoxville. Her organizational research focuses on the ways language and cultural factors impact people's organizational experiences. Specifically, she studies how leaders in geographically dispersed organizations use language to create unity and identification, student language choices impact their collegiate interactions, and how instructor messages impact students' educational experiences. She has published articles in *Journal of Applied Communication Research, Human Communication Research,* and *Communication Education.* With Astrid Sheil, she coauthored *Dynamic Public Relations: The 24/7 PR Cycle.* She may be contacted at Violanti@utk.edu.

Elizabeth A. Williams (Ph.D., organizational communication, Purdue University) is an assistant professor in the Department of Communication Studies at Colorado State University. Her research interests focus on identification, leadership, and training in a variety of organizational contexts, including distributed teams, multiteam systems, organizations experiencing change, nonprofit organizations, and health organizations. Her work has been published in *Journal of Communication, Journal of Applied Communication Research, Communication Studies, Journal of Health Communication, Health Communication,* and various edited volumes. She has conducted communication workshops in a variety of corporate and academic settings, has been recognized for excellence in teaching, and in 2012 she was awarded the International Communication Association's W. Charles Redding Dissertation Award. She may be contacted at elizabeth.a.williams@colostate.edu.

Alaina C. Zanin (M.S., Murray State University) is a doctoral candidate in the Department of Communication at the University of Oklahoma. She researches leadership communication and organizational communication in unique organizational contexts (e.g., life enrichment groups, nontraditional organizations, sports teams). She specializes in structuration, sensemaking, and framing theories, as well as issues surrounding power, control, resistance, gender, and body work. Her dissertation is on the structuring processes of resistance and control within an athletic healthcare organization. She may be contacted at alaina.zanin@ou.edu.

Author Index

Topic Index